SPEAK UP
and
FIGHT

A survivor's fight for healing, justice,
and the power to be heard.

Kaylynne Venn

 FriesenPress

One Printers Way
Altona, MB R0G 0B0
Canada

www.friesenpress.com

ISBN
978-1-03-834532-5 (Hardcover)
978-1-03-834531-8 (Paperback)
978-1-03-834533-2 (eBook)

1. BIOGRAPHY & AUTOBIOGRAPHY, PERSONAL MEMOIRS

Distributed to the trade by The Ingram Book Company

Author's Note

I want to dedicate this book to everyone who has ever been a victim or a survivor of any kind of sexual violence. I want each and every victim and survivor in this world to know that what happened to them was not their fault in any way, and they are not to blame for what truly happened. You did not deserve it in any way, and I know you did not ask for it.

No one has the right to ever harm you or make you feel uncomfortable, but I want you to know that you have the right to speak out and fight for what you believe. You have the right to use your voice. You do not have to keep suffering in silence. Your voice is the most powerful thing you have in your control right now. It took me almost a year and a half to find my voice and to be honest, I wish it didn't take that long; but now that I have it, I will never stay silent.

Because of this, I am writing this book to share my story, which is not an easy story to talk about; but it is my hope that I can inspire or even help victims and survivors of sexual violence know that there is hope. Still today, it's hard for me to acknowledge the fact that I am a rape survivor.

However this book isn't just to talk about how life knocked me down—I wrote it to show what it means to rise—to show the fight it takes to keep going when giving up feels easier. This isn't just a story of pain; it's a story of power. Of choosing to stand back up, reclaim my voice, and prove that even in our darkest moments, getting back up is still possible.

TABLE OF CONTENTS

Part 3

Trigger Warning

My story wasn't easy to live through, and I know it won't be easy to read as I share my experiences with rape, self-harm, suicide, and other difficult topics. However, I want this book to inspire others who have experienced something similar to what I did. There is a list of crisis lines at the back of the book. Please don't hesitate to reach out. If you're struggling, you are not alone.

INTRODUCTION

I was forced to go to hell, and I will never forget the countless days I spent fighting against my own mind just to stay alive. I endured a kind of suffering that will always stay with me— a pain so deep I buried it within myself.

It wasn't just physical; it left lasting scars on my mind. As a result of the rape, I never felt like a normal teenager. In a sense, I felt that part of my youth had been taken from me.

In 2018, I became a survivor, along with many others, but not by choice. Before I knew it, my old self had already left me, and a new one had officially started. I had said goodbye to everything I had ever cared about and everything I had ever planned to do or become. I prefer using the term 'survivor' rather than the term 'victim'.

I survived unthinkable struggles just to be here today, and I'm still standing because I have a goal: to speak out about my experience, share my story with others who haven't yet found their voice, and spread awareness about sexual violence. I was given the title 'the rape victim' after I was raped. You learn to try and hide yourself after being raped. It made me afraid to exist, wishing I could disappear.

I've learned that shame can unbelievably damage a person. No one wants to be remembered for the horrific things that occurred in their lives.

I feared that the title rape victim would haunt me for the rest of my life if I shared what had happened. I did not want to be known as a rape victim. But society says I'm a victim because that's the most commonly used word after a traumatic event, but not everyone agrees with the word victim.

For me, the word victim reminds me of the hell I've been through, while the word survivor reminds me that I've made it out alive, and I'm here today sharing my story—for survivors, for victims, for anyone who needs to hear it—to say that things will improve, things will get better because I know there is hope. My goal in speaking out is to show that there is a way out of the darkness that follows sexual violence.

PART 1

To him, "no" meant nothing.

Because of that, my life shattered into pieces,
dragging me into a private hell I never imagined.

But it wasn't forever, as I had imagined.

CHAPTER 1

The Beginning

Growing up, we tend to believe that nothing awful will ever happen to us—that our lives won't change in the blink of an eye, and that what happens to other people will never happen to us. Well, that's what I believed—until it happened.

For as long as I can remember, I've been a fighter. When I was younger, I struggled to speak properly due to a speech impairment. I also had difficulty putting my thoughts into words. At an early age, I was diagnosed with epilepsy, and I had to fight to accept that reality. I also had to fight to stand up for myself after being bullied because of my seizures and my difficulty reading and writing due to a learning disability. At age seven, I thought I might be fighting for my life when doctors suspected I had a brain tumour. After many hospital visits, they discovered it wasn't cancer, but a lesion on my brain that caused my seizures.

It always felt like I had to fight for everything. I fought to make the people who cared about me proud, and to prove the ones who doubted me wrong. That constant need to push myself is what fuelled my passion for Taekwondo. It was a sport that consumed my thoughts and brought out the fighter inside me—until my life was shattered.

My memory begins here: on a Friday in November 2018. I lived with both my parents and our dog. I'm an only child. There are some good things about that, but most of the time, I hated it. I spent a lot of time alone, either training in the basement or studying in my room. The day before, I had studied hard for an upcoming science test.

It was my first year of high school, and I knew how important my grades were—scoring below 50% meant failing. In middle school, I didn't put in my best effort, mostly because of stress from girl drama and how differently teachers treated me because of my learning disabilities. But high school felt like a fresh start. The teachers didn't make me feel different, and for the first time in a long time, I was motivated. I wanted to prove myself and show everyone what I was capable of achieving.

So, I set a goal: to focus completely on my education. I distanced myself from most of my friends to avoid drama and distractions. But I stayed close to my best friend Taylor. My alarm went off at 5:50 a.m., like it did every school day. Most people would think that's too early, especially since I didn't need to get ready until 7:30. But even though I wasn't a morning person, I forced myself out of bed and into the basement to train. There was no better feeling than being up before the sun, working to improve myself while the rest of the world slept.

Around 7:00 a.m., just as I was finishing training, I heard my phone buzz. A text from Noah lit up my screen: "Hey, would you like to hang out after school? I'd enjoy it if we could spend time together outside of school."

I replied, "I'll get back to you on that," and set my phone aside as I got ready for the day.

I'd met Noah during a lunch hour at school. I was sitting alone, eating and finishing some homework, when he came up to me. "Do you mind if I sit here?" he asked.

Despite my plan to keep to myself and focus on school, I replied softly, "I don't mind." We ended up talking for the rest of lunch. From then on, we gradually became friends.

As the school year went on, he chatted with me every morning at my locker. We shared inside jokes, went to the school gym after discovering we both liked fitness, and sometimes sat outside together during lunch.

But we never hung out outside of school. That was something I felt good about. I was always busy with schoolwork and Taekwondo—and truthfully, I had never spent time alone with a boy before.

My life was steady. Predictable. Structured. Until that morning at school. Noah walked up to my locker. "So, have you made up your mind yet? You didn't get back to my text."

"I'm sorry, I got caught up getting ready. If I said yes, what would we do?"

"We could go to free swim."

I felt more comfortable knowing a lot of people from school would be at the community pool—it was a popular Friday night hangout since it was free. "I guess... why not?" I said. He smiled wide when I agreed.

During first period, I had science class. I was relieved—it meant I could finally take the test I'd studied for. As soon as the bell rang, our teacher handed out the papers. I worked through the questions confidently, proud of what I'd prepared for. After double-checking everything, I handed it in.

There were about twenty minutes left in class, so I reviewed some math notes—my weakest subject. I noticed our science teacher grading the tests at her desk. After a while, she got up and approached one of the students, but before that, she paused by me and whispered, "Good job. You should be proud of yourself."

I smiled. "Thank you." All the effort had been worth it. The rest of the school day passed slowly, but it was a good day. I walked out to the parking lot and got in my mom's car, feeling proud and relieved.

"How was school?" she asked.

"It was good. Would it be okay if I went to free swim tonight with a friend?"

"Who?" she asked.

"Noah. I haven't told you about him, but we've been hanging out since September."

She paused, then said, "I don't see a problem with that. He can come over, and you guys can walk there together since it's close." Later that evening, I called Noah to make a plan. He asked if it was okay to bring a friend. I didn't mind, so we agreed to meet at my house around 6:30. When he arrived, he was alone. No friend.

I didn't think much of it. I grabbed my things and we headed out toward the pool. But swimming was never on his agenda. As I was forcefully pulled into a family changing room, everything became a blur.

CHAPTER 2

You'll Never Be Forgiven

I felt numb, as if my emotions had deserted me. Immediately, my chest tightened, and my breaths became shallow as I was pinned to the ground. He reached into his bathing suit pocket, pulled out a pocketknife, and held it up to my face, the blade shining in the light. "Don't make a sound," he warned. I couldn't help it as tears streamed down my face, begging him to stop, but it was all worthless. "Shut up!" he said as he traced a line down my stomach with the pocketknife.

I felt numb because I was in such a state of shock, but somehow it was like I could drown in the darkness of my own thoughts. As the darkness overpowered me, it felt as if there was no air around me.

I fought desperately to shift my focus away from the unfolding horror, searching for any distant thought to cling to. In my mind, I imagined waves crashing in from the sea onto the shoreline, and I imagined that each wave represented a different thought going through my mind. The noise of everyone shouting and splashing around in the community pool in the other room made me wish I wasn't who I was; instead, I wished I could be someone else.

My thoughts were racing in every direction at once, and many of them made no sense to me. I had no idea what was happening to me. How could someone have so many thoughts in their head at the same time? My mind felt both empty and full. *What the hell just happened to me?* That thought kept running through my mind again.

I was aware of the fact that what had happened was wrong and that it should never have taken place, but I was unable to come to terms with the fact that a real crime had been committed.

SEXUAL ASSAULT?? RAPE!

I was left lying on the cold, damp floor after the weight of his body had been lifted off mine, finally allowing me to breathe. I looked at him as our eyes met, and I felt my body become lifeless and my mind blank. "Put your bathing suit back on and get the fuck out of here," he said softly, gritting his teeth as his face burned with a redness that made me wonder what I had done to make him so angry.

He slowly opened the door and left, leaving me alone. It felt like my chest was closing up, and my whole body was shaking. I had a terrible feeling that I was going to pass out in there. I was aware there were people nearby. I could hear voices just outside the door. Too fearful he might come back and hurt me further, I didn't scream for help. Instead, I whispered to myself, "Help me."

The door unexpectedly pushed open, and a sudden gust of anxiety washed over me. I was already ashamed of the fact that someone had seen my naked, lifeless body. I couldn't bear the thought of a complete stranger seeing me in such a state. However, as soon as my eyes focused, I realized it was him. "What the bloody hell did I fucking say to you? You must get out right now, or else you won't want to know what's about to take place!" Fear struck through my body. It seemed like he expected me to just get up and act as if nothing was wrong. But how?

I tried to focus my mind on the things around me, attempting to calm my racing thoughts. On the right, just behind me, were a couple of lockers where personal belongings could be stored, and on the left was a restroom stall near a sink. But as soon as I took a deep breath, I glanced down at the floor between my legs and couldn't tear my eyes away from the red smear across the floor. In a state of disbelief, it took me a moment to realize it had come from me. It was my blood.

My stare was interrupted by three loud knocks at the door. "Are you going to be done in there soon?" he called.

"Yeah," I responded, my voice shaking. My chest felt heavy, and I had the sensation of drowning. Both of these feelings made my heart race, especially as I stared at the smeared blood in front of me. Nearing the point of passing out, I reached for my bathing suit that he had ripped off, hoping it was still wearable enough to put back on. The banging on the door continued, and with each knock, I wanted to run and hide—but there was nowhere to go.

At the same time, I couldn't stay in the changing room any longer, knowing I had been on the ground for what seemed like hours, trapped in unbearable suffering and pain, unable to speak for fear of my life. I was terrified he would stab me with the pocketknife he had been holding. I slowly shifted my weight from one foot to the next, moving closer to the door while keeping my balance against the wall. My hand reached for the door, but I froze when I saw, to my left, a mirror hanging over the sink. I didn't recognize myself. I worried that everyone would look at me and know that I wasn't okay.

My eyes stared back at me from the reflection as I fought to hold back tears. I walked away from the door and stood directly in front of the mirror, looking myself dead-on in the eyes, whispering to myself, "You have to be strong." After taking a few deep breaths, I reached for the door handle and opened it.

He was standing not far from the changing room as I walked out. I couldn't make eye contact with the boy I once called a close friend. I wondered what he would see if he looked me in the eye. I was ashamed of my vulnerability and filled with anger. But more than that, I wondered if he would see that the person I had been was no longer there. He now owned that part of me, and for that, I hated him.

I finally looked him in the eye as he stood there, almost completely acting like nothing had happened. Suddenly, a wave of rage rushed through my body, and I felt like I was about to explode in anger. "Get the hell out of here!" I gasped through clenched teeth.

"Alright, whatever you want, babe. You don't have to speak to me like that," he replied. *Didn't he know what he'd done to me?* That thought flashed through my mind. The look on his face made it seem like he was angry at me. I didn't care. I could have said much worse to him, and in reality, I wished I had. He deserved it.

"Remember, if you tell anybody, I'll hurt you." That was the last thing he said to me that day as he left. An indescribable fear washed over me, a fear of not telling anyone. Even if he hadn't said those exact words, I still had the feeling that nobody would believe me—after all, no one saw what happened behind the closed door.

Nothing happened. I tried my best to convince myself as I rushed to the bathroom, hoping no one would see me. I walked as fast as I could. When I got there, I took a closer look in the mirror and noticed my eyes were red and swollen from crying. My hair, which had been in a tight bun, was now a mess, and fingernail marks were dug into my neck.

I tried to regain control of my anxiety as quickly as possible by taking slow, deep breaths and splashing some cold water on my face. I redid my hair and pulled it back into a tight bun, throwing on my clothes while doing my best to hide the fingernail marks on my body, hoping my parents wouldn't see.

I pushed open the doors to the outside and ran out of the community pool. As I did, a gust of wind and snow hit me, the cold air biting at my skin. I gasped as the chill rushed into my lungs, snapping me back to reality and giving me a level of awareness that had been absent before. Despite not wanting to think about it, I now knew for certain what had really happened.

14

I walked home, which only took about five minutes. Dropping my bag in the kitchen, I heard my parents call from the living room. "Did you have fun at the pool?" my mom asked, looking at me.

"Yeah, I had fun," I replied, trying to sound convincing.

"That's good to hear. Did you know that Noah came to the door to ask for a plastic bag for his bathing suit?" my dad said.

"No, I didn't know that," I answered, unsure of what to think. *Why the hell would he come here?* I questioned myself.

"Well, I hope you don't mind that I drove him home since it was snowing and cold outside."

I stood there, shocked, not sure how to feel or what to think. But I made an effort to hide my emotions—I didn't want my parents to wonder why I was upset. It wasn't my dad's fault; he was just trying to be nice. The thought twisted inside me—my dad had just driven my rapist home, unknowingly giving him kindness he never deserved.

"Well, anyway, I'm going for a shower," I said, trying to leave before my emotions could show. I hoped that a shower would help me somehow wash away the anxiety and pain that had already taken hold of me. I scrubbed the soap harshly against my skin, my movements growing faster with each passing moment. The fear of never feeling clean enough consumed me. But it went deeper than that—the thought of him being inside of me made me feel nauseous, sick to my stomach.

I let the water run over me, hoping it would calm my racing mind. But one thought stood out, clear and cold like a deep blue sky with no haze: *My life is forever over.* I let the water flow over me, trying to wash away the feeling of his body against mine. But it lingered, even after I turned the hot water up high enough to make my skin burn.

It felt like a terrifying horror movie, where the same few scenes played over and over again. These images kept cycling through my mind: his hands rubbing my body, how he forced himself inside of me, the smell of cigarettes clinging to his bathing suit and breath,

15

the words he said to me, the image of the knife, and the weight of his body pressing down on mine, making it hard to breathe.

I walked out of the shower with red, swollen skin, sore to the touch. I changed into my pajamas, crawled into bed, and closed my eyes as tightly as I could, pulling the covers around me in an attempt to feel safe. The silence in the room, as I tried to sleep, only made things worse.

He had taken away both my power and my sense of who I used to be, and I couldn't stop thinking about it. He was the last person I wanted to think about, yet I couldn't escape him.

My memory of what actually happened after he held the knife to my throat, scratched a line down my stomach and threatened to kill me was difficult to piece together. It was too painful to process and far beyond my ability to fully understand, let alone replay the horrifying event in my mind.

I don't remember getting any sleep that night; instead, I tossed and turned, tears running down my cheeks, wondering why life had to be so unfair.

CHAPTER 3

Dark Thoughts

I had no idea how long I'd been lying there that Saturday morning, staring blankly at the ceiling. Minutes? Hours? Time felt frozen. A noise rang out from somewhere outside, sharp and sudden—but I couldn't bring myself to move. I didn't want to know what it was. I stayed still, emotionally paralyzed, deciding that the less I interacted with anyone, the easier it would be to keep my secret hidden.

I'm to blame. That thought ran on a loop in my mind, convincing me I had somehow let him treat me that way. "I'm a victim now, and I can't go back and change it," I whispered to myself. Deep down, I knew what had happened. I had been raped. But I couldn't say the word out loud—because if I did, it would become real. I was nothing more than an innocent 14-year-old girl—someone who had never had a boyfriend, never experienced sex, and had no desire for either of them. The thought that I had been raped took up a significant part of my mind, yet I did not want to accept it as a fact.

The longer I stayed in bed, the more time stretched—each second pulling me deeper into the weight of my thoughts. The memories pressed in, relentless and suffocating. Finally, I swung my legs over the edge of the bed and forced myself to stand. The truth was bitter and unshakable: my old life was gone. But I had to keep moving, even if it was just to step outside, feel the air on my skin, and remind myself that the world still existed beyond my pain.

I walked around the neighbourhood near my home, letting the wind brush against my face. It helped clear my mind—just like it had the day before. For a brief moment, I felt present. But the clearer my mind became, the deeper I was pulled back into my thoughts. As much as I didn't want to be trapped in the past, I didn't want to be in the present either.

One thought echoed like it was written in bold across my mind: *My life is forever over. I will always be a victim.* And in that moment, it felt painfully true. I watched several cars drive by, and it felt like life had moved on without me. People were heading to work, going to school, spending time with friends and family, and returning to their homes at the end of the day—just living. But the rest of my life seemed to be happening without me in it, and I had no idea how to cope with that.

Remember, you tell anybody, I'll hurt you. Those words kept replaying in my mind, over and over again. It was like he was yelling inside my head. His voice became a recurring nightmare I couldn't escape. A part of me wanted to speak out—I even thought about going to the police. But it had all happened behind closed doors. No witnesses. No proof. Why would anyone believe me?

"If anything ever happens that doesn't feel right, you can always come talk to us." My parents had said that to me countless times growing up—and they still do. They always reassured me they'd be there, no matter what life threw my way. That I could come to them with anything. But I couldn't find the words to tell them I had been raped. No parent wants to hear those words from their child. And I truly believed it was my fault—maybe I had done something to make him think it was okay. Worst of all, I hadn't even fought back.

As I stood watching the cars pass by, someone suddenly bumped into me. They were glued to their phone, not paying attention to anything around them. "I'm so sorry," they said quickly before walking off, eyes already back on their screen. I stood frozen. My heart pounded. My breathing turned shallow, and my body tensed as a wave of anxiety hit me out of nowhere. I felt like I might pass out—or throw up. But I ignored it and kept walking, pretending I was fine.

I was never someone who could keep secrets from my parents. But this was different. I didn't have the strength to say what had happened. It felt like my mouth was duct-taped shut—words trapped behind silence—as his voice echoed in my head: *You tell, I'll hurt you.* Over and over again. "Shut up!" I yelled out loud, trying to silence them. But I couldn't find a way out of my own mind. I was stuck in an endless cycle of fear and shame, searching for reasons to stay quiet.

I kept walking, trying to clear my thoughts, when suddenly a car horn blared. I froze. My body tensed with fear. I didn't understand why every little sound in the outside world made me feel like I was under attack. I turned to see what was happening—but there was nothing there. Still, the noise had pulled me back into the moment. And for a second, everything in my head went quiet. As I focused on the road ahead, a terrifying thought crept in—one I had never had before. I didn't want to think it, but I didn't know what else to do.

I walked slowly toward the edge of the road. The cars rushed past, and the wind whipped against my body like it was holding me upright. I told myself that maybe this was the answer. That maybe I could finally be free from the chains of my trauma. "This won't affect me anymore," I whispered. Thoughts flooded my mind faster than I could process them. And as I edged closer, something strange happened—my mind began pulling me back. One by one, memories surfaced. It was like flipping through the pages of a picture book—snapshots of joy, of safety, of life before all of this.

I began thinking about all the people, places, and moments that used to make me happy. But no matter what I tried to focus on, my mind kept circling back to one thing—my passion. The one thing that had brought me more joy and purpose than anything else—Taekwondo.

It had given me confidence, discipline, and strength. It filled my life with meaningful memories. And yet, in the days after the rape, I did everything I could to block it out of my mind completely. I hated myself for not stopping him. I couldn't understand how, after spending seven years learning to defend myself, I wasn't able to stop what happened. I was furious with myself. It felt like everything I had learned disappeared the moment I needed it most. I froze completely—like a deer in headlights.

In my mind, I could see the exact moment I had decided to take Taekwondo as far as I possibly could. I loved competing, and that love pushed me to become more disciplined, to shape my body into something stronger. What began as two classes a week for five years turned into three classes a week when I was twelve. I knew that if I wanted to succeed in this sport, I had to give it everything I had. I also trained in Taekwondo at home on my own for a couple of hours each week. Over time, I finally began to improve. By the age of 14, I had the skills to defend myself. I was still raped. My body and mind did not perform the way I wanted it to; the fact that I knew how to defend myself and get away from that situation did not prevent me from becoming a rape victim.

I remember that just a few days before the rape, I came across a post on social media about the benefits of martial arts for women—and why more women should get involved. The message focused on self-defence, on learning how to protect yourself from sexual violence. It claimed that martial arts could prepare you for anything the world might throw at you.

But my mind couldn't. It froze. Everything I had worked so hard for—everything I had trained to do—disappeared in that moment. Nobody talks about what happens when the person who attacks you is someone you already know. Your body can be trained to fight—but this wasn't the fight I had been preparing for. I could punch and kick in a ring, but nothing prepared me for how my mind and body would shut down in the face of something I never imagined could happen to me.

As I stood by the side of the road, it hit me—I had no idea how to live my life anymore. And just like that, the blame turned inward. *I wouldn't be in this fucking mess if I had just fought back,* I thought. Drowning in misery, I inched closer to the flow of traffic— until thoughts of the people who cared about me began to surface. The ones who loved me. The ones who would miss me terribly— my parents,

In my head, I heard a voice scream, *What would my parents do if I were gone?* I couldn't stop thinking about it. How could I put them through that kind of pain? How had I let myself become someone who could even think about doing this?

I shook my head, as if I could force the suicidal thoughts out— make them leave for good. My eyes filled with tears as I turned and walked back down the sidewalk, heading toward a nearby park where I could sit on a bench and breathe.

The thought of living through another day feeling this broken, this disgusted with myself, was unbearable. After a long, lonely walk, I decided it was time to go home. I opened the door without saying a word to my parents and headed straight downstairs. I just needed to be alone. To breathe. To exist without being seen.

My mind kept circling back to suicidal thoughts—and that terri- fied me. I didn't want to die. I just didn't want to feel trapped in my past anymore. It felt like I had no control over my own thoughts.

I started pacing the room in frustration, my body restless with anger. *How was it possible for me to be so completely unaware of the fact that he planned to rape me?*

As I walked back and forth, anger and confusion churned in my chest. *Is there even a good explanation for why he crossed that line?* I wondered. I couldn't understand how anyone—any human being—could be capable of doing something so violent.

Did he even realize what this was doing to me? How deeply it was destroying parts of me I didn't even know existed? My thoughts started racing so fast, I just wanted them to stop.

Then a memory surfaced. I was in seventh grade when I first heard girls at school talk about cutting. I didn't get it. Honestly, I thought they were just doing it for attention. But later, curiosity got the better of me. I searched: Why do people self-harm? I clicked on the first link. Over and over, I saw the same answer—it's a way to cope.

I took a deep breath, whispering, "Don't do it... this is stupid." But that didn't stop me. That day, I picked up a blade for the first time in my life—and used it in a way it was never meant to be used. The second I did it, I knew it was a terrible decision. But there was no taking it back.

Cutting became the only thing that seemed to numb the pain I was in. The anger. The sadness. The self-hate. For a moment, it all went quiet. It felt like the only thing keeping me from completely falling apart. But the more I cut, the more I needed it. The relief didn't last long. And soon, it became something I craved.

Before I knew it, I was staring at my arm, covered in lines. Each cut felt like a physical reflection of how broken, angry, and disgusted I felt inside. Then reality hit me. *Fuck. Why did I do this to myself? My parents are going to hate me. They'll think I'm just doing this for attention.* Now I had two secrets to hide—what happened to me the day he raped me, and the reason I had cut across my whole arm.

The anxiety and fear became unbearable. I started to realize that even though cutting helped for a moment, it was also something else—something dangerous. It was becoming a habit. An escape I was scared of needing. I thought about going to school on Monday and seeing him. The thought made my chest tighten. I couldn't breathe. And then I imagined my parents finding me—on the ground, my arms bleeding, unable to move. That image made my heart race even faster. *I can't handle this anymore.* That thought kept repeating in my head like a drumbeat.

I told myself that maybe if I went to bed early, I could avoid hurting myself again. But sleep didn't feel safe either. The idea of reliving everything in a nightmare terrified me. Still, I knew I had to sleep eventually. I rolled down my sleeves to hide the cuts and walked upstairs. I passed my parents in the hallway and said goodnight. It was only 9:00 p.m. As I got into bed, another thought crept in— *I hope when I fall asleep, I won't wake up.*

CHAPTER 4

Screaming For Help

Getting out of bed had never been something I truly struggled with—until the night I was raped. After that, everything changed. My mind was full of images of the person I used to be, and I couldn't understand how it had all fallen apart so quickly. Before high school, mornings weren't always easy. Some days, I didn't want to get out of bed. But I always did—because of Taekwondo. Training at home gave me purpose and routine. It was equal parts passion and pressure, but I never missed a day.

If I wanted to achieve my goals, I had to push through the discomfort. That discipline had always grounded me. But after the rape, everything changed. Monday came. The day I had feared. My alarm was still set for 5:50 a.m., but instead of dragging myself out of bed like I used to, I turned it off and went back to sleep. My mom's voice eventually broke through. "Why are you not out of bed yet?" she asked, flicking on the bedroom light.

I buried my face in the pillow. "I'm not feeling well. I want to stay home."

I knew she didn't believe me. I'd used that excuse before. I had always struggled with school—not the learning part, but the bullying. Still, this wasn't about school anymore. This was different. But my excuses didn't work. I pulled myself out of bed and threw on whatever clothes were closest, not even caring if they matched. My only goal was to hide the wounds—both the ones I had created and the cut across my stomach from his knife.

I walked most of the way to school, dragging my bag behind me, sick to my stomach. The thought of seeing him made my skin crawl. Each step toward that building felt heavier than the last. The doors creaked open and I stepped into the crowd. The noise, the movement, the number of people—it overwhelmed me. I froze. Everyone around me looked so normal, like nothing had changed. And yet, I was falling apart.

I walked to my locker to grab my binder, feeling completely alone despite being surrounded by hundreds of people. That's the most isolating feeling—being in a crowd and knowing no one has any idea what you're going through. No one knew I had nearly ended my life. No one knew my arms were covered in cuts. I was suffocating in silence.

Then Taylor, one of my friends, walked up to me. "So, I hear you have a boyfriend now."

I blinked. "What are you talking about?"

"Noah posted on all his socials that you two are dating."

"What the hell? We're not dating. We're not even friends anymore."

She raised an eyebrow. "Then why would he post that?"

The doubt in her face stung. "Come with me," I said, pulling her into the washroom. I rolled up my sleeves, looked her in the eye, and said, "I did all of this because of him." The bell rang.

Taylor backed away. "I have to go," she said quickly—and left without asking anything else. I stood there, staring into the mirror. A single tear slid down my cheek.

"She better not tell anyone," I whispered, wiping it away and heading to class.

In science class, I noticed she wasn't there. I sat in the far corner, head down, arms wrapped tightly around myself. My chest was tight. My whole body was shaking. And then Taylor walked in. She walked straight to me. "The guidance counselor is waiting outside. She wants to talk to you."

My stomach dropped. "I didn't want you to tell anyone," I whispered, standing up with anger and fear burning in my throat. I stepped out into the hallway, arms crossed to hide my sleeves.

"Hey, Kaylynne," the guidance counsellor said gently. "Can we talk in my office?" The second the door closed, my anxiety exploded. "I had a little chat with Taylor about what's on your arms," she said. "Do you want to talk to me about it?"

"No," I answered, eyes glued to the floor.

"Have you told your parents?"

I shook my head. "No. They don't know."

"I know this is hard," she said. "But by law, I have to inform them. I'm really sorry."

"Please don't," I begged. "They'll be mad. They won't understand." But nothing I said could stop it. She made the call. When I got home, my heart was pounding. I kept playing out every possible reaction in my mind. *They'll scream. They'll think I'm crazy. They'll never trust me again.*

But when I walked through the door, my mom just looked at me and said, "Don't ever do that to yourself again." And then—silence. Confusion. Shock. They didn't understand. I think they just didn't know what to do with the version of me they had just discovered. They weren't angry. They weren't cold. They were just... frozen. Like they were trying to process who I had become, while I was still trying to figure that out myself.

My mom took me to the doctor, hoping someone else could give her answers she didn't know how to find. I sat in the office, staring at the floor, barely hearing the words being said. And then it came: severe depression. That was the diagnosis. The label. But it felt too small for what was happening inside me. It wasn't just about feeling sad or unmotivated. It wasn't just about crying myself to sleep or losing interest in things I used to love. It was about waking up and feeling like I didn't belong in my own skin. It was about wanting to disappear—but not knowing how to explain that to anyone. It was about keeping secrets so heavy, they made my whole body ache.

They called it depression, but I knew it was more than that. Still, I didn't argue. I let them put a name on it. I let them hand me a prescription and pretend it was a solution. Because at that point, even a name—*any* name—felt better than continuing to live inside this unnamed storm. On the drive home, I sat in silence, staring out the window. People were walking their dogs, getting groceries, talking on their phones—just living. And all I could think was, *I wish I could be someone else.* Anyone but me.

After the diagnosis, my mom spoke to the guidance counsellor again. Soon, most of my teachers were informed. I was allowed to leave class and talk to someone if I was struggling. But I stopped making eye contact with people. I stopped talking to my friends. I stopped talking, period.

I still let people see the version of me they expected—the cheerful, outgoing, put-together girl. But it was just a mask. One I had to wear to survive. And the moment someone got too close to seeing the real me, I shut them out completely.

Because I was terrified they'd see just how broken I really was.

CHAPTER 5

Should Have Kept My Mouth Shut

When I was in middle school, there was a poster on the wall in the school office. It said, "School is a safe place for everyone to learn." I believed that—school should be a safe space. But in Grade 9, I learned that for some of us, school could be anything but.

There was nowhere to hide from him. I stopped going to class and spent my days wandering the halls, trying to disappear. But he always found me. He'd press his arm around my shoulder and whisper threats in my ear: "Come with me. If you don't remember, I know where you live, and I will hurt you." He meant it. Every day since the night he raped me, he would drag me to the back of the school while most students were in class. He'd pin me to the outside wall and grope me until someone came around the corner or the bell rang. I tried to fight back. But every time I did, he reminded me that he had a knife and he was the one in control.

I had reached my limit. I couldn't take another day of his hands on me. I knew I needed to speak up. I couldn't tell my parents—not after how they reacted to my self-harm. So I decided to go to the guidance counselor. She already knew part of my truth. Maybe she'd believe the rest.

That Monday, I walked through the school doors paralyzed by fear. I didn't know what I would say or how I'd even begin. When the bell rang, I forced myself to the guidance office. I knocked, barely able to speak. "Can I talk to you?" I asked.

She welcomed me in. I sat down and stared at the floor as my hands trembled. "Noah touched me inappropriately," I said quietly. "I told him to stop, but he didn't listen."

Her response hit like a slap. "Boys will be boys. He must have liked you."

I stared at her, stunned. That was it? That was her answer? My fists clenched. My whole body burned with rage. Was this supposed to be normal? If it was, why did I feel so broken? Why couldn't I sleep? Why was I cutting myself just to breathe?

I shot up from the chair, voice shaking with fury. "What happened was not right." Then I walked out before I exploded.

I stormed down the hall and collapsed by the gym doors, my back pressed to the wall. I pulled my hood over my head, curled up, and tried to breathe. My arms wrapped around my head like a shield. I didn't want anyone to see me cry. I didn't want anyone to see me at all. If she didn't believe me, who would?

I sat there through lunch—silent, invisible, shattered. Then I felt it. A firm grip on my arm.

"Come with me, and don't make a big scene," he whispered. I looked up. Noah. His eyes were cold. "I have a knife in my backpack." My breath caught. Everything in me froze. My body wouldn't move, but my legs did anyway. I followed him—numb, terrified—through the hallway, past crowds of students. None of them saw the fear on my face.

I thought he was taking me outside again. But he brought me into a staff washroom.

He locked the door, dropped his backpack, and stepped in front of it. "What did I tell you about not saying anything?" he growled, slamming me against the wall.

"I didn't say anything, I promise," I choked out.

"Then why the hell did the guidance counsellor talk to me?" he shouted.

"I don't know! I'm sorry!" I snapped, angry and scared. She hadn't told me she was going to talk to him. She never took me seriously— so why would she act like she cared now?

I didn't understand. I felt confused and betrayed.

He backed away, and I thought for a second that he might leave. Instead, he pulled out his knife—and something else. A needle. "Do you want me to kill you in here?" he said, pointing it at me.

Tears streamed down my face. I couldn't breathe. "What are you going to do with that?"

"It depends," he said, smirking. "If you listen, you don't have to worry about it."

It was like my soul left my body. I collapsed to the ground, numb. He climbed on top of me and wrapped his arms around me, holding me down. I tried to fight. He held my wrists above my head. With one hand, he stripped off my shirt—then everything else.

He raped me. Again.

He left before the bell rang. I ran through the hallways, a teacher calling after me, but I didn't stop. I ran to my locker, grabbed my bag, and sprinted home. I didn't look both ways before crossing the street. My mom looked confused. "Why are you home?" I didn't answer. I locked myself in my room. She knocked. "Are you okay?"

"Just leave me alone!" Eventually, she did.

I collapsed on the floor, sobbing until I couldn't cry anymore. I didn't want to think. I didn't want to feel. I found a blade and carved fresh wounds into my arms. I just wanted the pain to stop. I didn't have words for any of it. My life had become a nightmare I couldn't wake up from. Around 3:30 p.m., I heard a knock. My heart stopped.

"Noah's at the door," my mom called. My heart dropped. My chest tightened. I couldn't breathe. Panic flooded me, but I didn't know what to say. What excuse to make. What to do.

I grabbed a hoodie to hide the cuts and wiped my face, trying to pull myself together—trying to look normal. But inside, I was falling apart.

I opened my bedroom door. And there he was. After he found out my address, Noah started showing up almost every day. My parents thought it was innocent—just a friend from school. They didn't see the way my hands shook when I heard the doorbell. They didn't see how I begged them, sometimes in whispers, "Can you just tell him I'm not home?" And sometimes they did.

But I stopped asking as much. I didn't want them to get suspicious. So I stayed quiet.

This time, I didn't say anything. I just walked out, shutting the door behind me. My legs felt like lead. Every step felt like a trap.

Then he shoved me against the stucco wall. And assaulted me again—right there, at my own house.

My body went numb. My limbs wouldn't move. I wanted to scream, but nothing came out. I froze. My body betrayed me. Again.

When he left, my parents asked, "Why doesn't he stay long?" I had no answer. I didn't feel safe at school. I didn't feel safe at home. And no matter how hard I begged my parents to let me stay home, they still sent me to school. If I'd had a physical illness, they would have let me stay—but my pain was invisible, and they didn't know how to recognize it.

I started skipping class, hiding in hallways, or running out of the building. I couldn't focus. I stopped caring. My grades dropped. I wore baggy clothes to hide myself. I hated who I was. I didn't want to live.

I blamed myself. I felt disgusted. I believed I didn't matter. And even though my parents said they noticed something had changed in me—that they were concerned—I didn't want their help. Because I didn't believe anyone could save me.

CHAPTER 6

Psych Ward

On December 14th, 2018, I wasn't in class—I was wandering the school hallways, lost in thought. I couldn't focus, couldn't pretend, couldn't breathe right. The suicidal thoughts had only gotten worse. My mind was stuck on one thing: dying. I didn't want to feel this way anymore. I didn't want to feel *anything* anymore. I just wanted peace, even if that meant no longer being here.

As I turned the corner, I saw him—Noah. My stomach dropped. Before he could spot me, I bolted out of the school doors. I wasn't sure if I was out of breath from running or from the sheer panic flooding my chest. The sun hit the snowy sidewalks as I paced along the side of the school, my boots crunching through the snow. The cold didn't matter. I felt nothing. Only the pain inside me registered—and it was all-consuming.

And then, as I walked with numbness settling in, I felt ready. Ready to take that final step and make the pain stop. I pulled out my phone. My hands trembled as I opened the "notes" app and looked at the goodbye message I had typed to my parents. But something made me scroll—and I stumbled across an old text from Taylor. *Kaylynne, I'm here for you. Please keep fighting.* She had sent it the day she saw my cuts. Her words felt like a small light in the dark. I stared at them for a while. Somehow, they gave me just enough strength to turn around and go back inside.

I was scared Noah would see me as I crept up the stairs toward the resource room, where I often spent time hiding from classes and crowds. I slipped inside and headed to the back table. It was packed with students catching up on work, but no one noticed me. No one ever did. No one saw the tears in my eyes. No one saw the way I was breaking. No one saw how close I was to leaving this world.

I was invisible—until the resource teacher sat across from me and asked how I was doing. I looked at her. Paused. Then I finally whispered, "I want to kill myself."

She stared. "Don't be silly."

I blinked. *Did she just say that?* Something in me snapped. Words poured out before I could stop them. "You don't understand. A guy touched me inappropriately. I told him to stop… he didn't." I hadn't even planned to say it. It just… came out.

She stood up and said, "It's fine. Boys will be boys. Get your work done so you can actually pass your class." Then she walked away. I was frozen. *What the fuck just happened?* I pulled out my phone, shaking with anger and pain, and texted my mom something no parent ever wants to read:

"**I can't do this anymore. I want to kill myself.**" I waited, staring at the screen through blurry eyes.

Finally, she replied. "**Do you want help?**"

"**I just feel helpless,**" I texted back.

Her next message came fast: "**Stay where you are. Dad and I are coming.**" They picked me up and took me straight to the emergency room. It was my first time in the hospital for my mental health. I rode in silence in the back seat, my head down, palms covering my eyes, trying to keep from crying.

I needed help so badly—but didn't believe anyone could help me. The people I trusted—my guidance counsellor, the resource teacher—had already shown me they didn't care. Why would anyone else?

When we walked into the ER, I felt like I didn't belong. I wasn't physically sick. I wasn't bleeding. I just wanted to die. When the triage nurse asked why I was there, I couldn't answer. I stared at the floor, frozen in shame.

My mom stepped in. "She's been having suicidal thoughts. She's also been diagnosed with severe depression."

The nurse's tone shifted, and so did her eyes. Suddenly, I wasn't a person anymore—I was a chart, a diagnosis, a case file. Her gaze turned clinical, distant, like I was just another kid wasting space in a real hospital.

I wanted to shrink. To disappear. To vanish from that chair completely. Eventually, I was brought to a room, but that didn't mean anything happened right away. I waited for hours—staring at the walls, watching time crawl by, trying not to think too much. The silence made everything feel worse.

It wasn't until around 10:30 p.m. that a psychiatrist finally came in to speak with me. His questions were calm and gentle, but I was cautious with every answer. I kept things vague—strategically quiet. I was terrified. If I told the truth about what Noah had done, my parents might find out. Maybe the police. Maybe Child and Family Services.

And if Noah ever found out I told someone… I knew he'd hurt me again. He'd already proven that. So I lied. I said I was just sad. That school was hard. That I'd been feeling off. Inside, I was screaming. *Of course there was a reason!* But saying it would make it real—and I didn't want it to be real. "I'm wondering if there's a reason you're feeling like this?" he asked.

"No," I answered.

He studied me quietly, flipping through the papers on his clipboard. Then he looked back at me. "Well," he said, "I think it would be best if we admitted you to the hospital tonight."

My stomach dropped. I didn't want to be locked away—but I also didn't want to keep living like this. I didn't know what the right choice was.

"I don't know what to do," I whispered.

"Let's admit you," he said gently. "We'll go from there."

A nurse entered the room an hour later. "We're taking you to the psych ward now," she said. I stood up slowly, nerves twisting in my chest. A security guard stood outside the door with a wheelchair.

"Want a ride?" he asked lightly. "It's a long walk."

"I'm fine," I said, arms crossed over my chest, eyes down. I didn't want anyone touching me. The walk really was long. We passed through endless underground corridors beneath the hospital, some dimly lit and eerily silent. I remember passing empty beds and wondering who else had walked this path before me.

When we reached the unit, the doors shut and locked behind us. I was officially admitted. The nurses wore everyday clothes and introduced themselves by first name. One of them—Chloe—led me into a small intake room. She was calm, kind. She took my vitals, asked how I was feeling, and gently explained they needed to check my body for anything I could use to hurt myself. My heart sank as she asked me to hand over my hoodie and my shoes. Each item—my shoes, my sweater—was placed into a bag, sealed with a hospital sticker. My name printed on the front.

Something about it made me feel like I was disappearing. She asked a final question: "How are things at home?"

I answered automatically: "Fine." But were they? I had two loving parents who wanted what was best for me. But I couldn't tell them what was really happening—how Noah kept showing up. How unsafe I felt in my own house. How every time the door knocked, my stomach dropped in fear.

So I stayed quiet. Because trauma taught me that silence was safer. The room they assigned me was cold and bare. A single bed with a thin blanket. A chair that was almost impossible to move. A locked closet. A window in the door so the nurses could check in. I lay there that first night, knees pulled to my chest, arms around myself. My parents had just left after visiting me. I could still hear the echo of my mom's voice in the hallway as she cried to the nurse. I bit my lip and squeezed my eyes shut, trying not to cry too. I didn't want this to be my life. I missed my room. My bed. I missed feeling like a person.

At some point, I fell asleep—only to wake up to shouting. Terrified, I ran to the door and cracked it open. Two security guards were restraining a patient who was screaming, "I'm going to kill you!" I froze. My heart pounded. My breath caught in my throat.

I dropped to the floor, shaking, and whispered to myself, *I want to go home. I need to leave. I want to escape.* Panic set in. Tears fell. I couldn't breathe. Then the thoughts came—dark, sudden, loud: *I should have killed myself when I had the chance.*

A nurse passing by heard me. She opened the door and approached slowly. "Hey," she said softly. "Come sit with me."

I nodded and sat on the bed beside her, tears still running. "This isn't supposed to be my life," I choked. "I'm not supposed to be here." She didn't tell me to be strong. She didn't rush me. She just sat with me and listened. It was the first time I felt like someone actually saw how deep the pain went.

She asked, "On a scale from 1 to 10, how strong are your suicidal thoughts right now?"

"An eight," I admitted. And somehow, being honest helped just enough to get me through the night. The next few days were quiet, but hard. I spent hours in my room. When I did talk to the psychiatrist, I stuck to the story I'd started—bullying. Sixth grade. Girl drama. It wasn't the truth, but it wasn't a lie either. It just wasn't the *real* reason. But I could tell the psychiatrist didn't fully buy it. I wasn't good at lying. They started blaming my brain. They looked at my epilepsy diagnosis and the lesion on my brain.

"Maybe that's why she's feeling this way," I overheard. I wanted to scream. *No, that's not it! I've lived with epilepsy my whole life.* But what I couldn't say was what *had* changed—what had broken me.

One night during my stay, Chloe came back on shift after a couple days and sat with me, just like she had before. "You won't feel this way forever," she said. "This pain isn't your whole life." I didn't believe her. Not yet. But I needed to hear it.

My parents came every day, trying to smile, trying to be strong for me. Back then, I couldn't see how hard this was for them too. But now, I know—those visits saved me. Their presence reminded me that someone still loved me when I couldn't love myself.

I was taught ways to cope with urges to self-harm. Snap an elastic. Hold an ice cube. Draw red lines instead of cutting. It all felt point-less at the time. My thoughts were so dark, so final. I didn't want *alternatives.* I wanted everything to stop. But I remembered the tools anyway. Maybe some part of me hoped I'd need them one day—if I ever wanted to live again.

After four days, the psychiatrist said I was stable enough to go home. I lied. I told them I felt better. I told them I wasn't suicidal anymore. They believed me. Or maybe they had to. I was under 18, and in our system, that meant my stay would only ever be temporary. They discharged me with papers and prescriptions—but no plan for what I really needed: safety, protection, someone who believed me.

I left the hospital with the same secret. The same pain. Only now, it was buried a little deeper.

CHAPTER 7

Helpless

When I returned home from the hospital, everything felt different. My parents were on edge—and I couldn't blame them. Just four days ago, they had learned that I wanted to end my life. Now, medication was hidden away. Sharp objects were locked up. The whole house felt like it was holding its breath.

They knew I was struggling with depression and self-harm, but I didn't think they truly understood just how serious I was about not wanting to be here anymore. It hurt to realize that even my family didn't see me the same way anymore. Their caution was understandable, but heartbreaking.

No parent should ever have to fear for their child's safety like mine now did. One morning, I woke up and realized this was my new normal. I was no longer in control of my own medication. Razors, scissors, knives—anything with a blade—had vanished from the house. It was like the world no longer trusted me to take care of myself.

Every time suicidal thoughts came back, it broke me a little more. I didn't want to leave my parents with the pain of losing me. But I also didn't want to live with the pain I carried in the aftermath of the rape. No one knew it yet, but the thoughts became constant. Unrelenting.

Eventually, they led me to sit down and make a plan. I told myself, *I'm not going to ruin Christmas for my parents.* That promise bought me some time—time to think, to delay, to wonder if I really wanted to go through with it. But even then, I wasn't sure I had the strength to keep holding on.

Some nights, I felt like I was trapped in a prison made of memories. I'd sit hunched over, my head buried in my hands, sobbing until my body gave out. I didn't recognize myself anymore. The girl I used to be felt like a stranger, someone I could barely remember.

One person had broken me so completely—and I couldn't understand how or why. A few days after I got home from the hospital, I sat alone in my room, crying, and started writing a letter to my parents.

But this wasn't just a letter—it was a suicide note. I felt so helpless, so lost, so convinced that death was the only way out. *The only escape is death,* I told myself. *There's no other way to get out of this hell.*

I kept the note close, tucked deep inside my school bag, just in case I ever found the 'right' moment. But one day at school, as I was digging through my bag, I realized it was gone. My heart dropped. I panicked. I had no idea where it had gone—until I heard someone call my name.

"Kaylynne, come over here; I need to speak to you." It was the resource teacher. She stood holding a neatly folded piece of paper. The second I saw it, I knew. My eyes widened. My heart started pounding. I froze as she approached me. "I need to have a conversation with you in private," she said gently.

I followed her down the hall, barely breathing, into a small room near the school office. She unfolded the letter and placed it on the table beside me. "What were you thinking when you wrote this?"

I stared at the paper, searching for an answer I didn't want to give. "I didn't write that," I lied. She didn't believe me. I could tell instantly.

"It's your handwriting," she said.

"Okay, well, where did you find it?"

"I found it on the ground near your classroom. But that's not the point. I'm really worried about your safety, and I need to get the guidance counsellor involved."

I felt sick. Angry at myself for ever bringing that letter to school. Ashamed that I'd dropped it. Relieved that no one else had found it first. But deep down, I knew what was coming. It had only been a few days since I was discharged from the hospital, and now I knew—I wasn't going home after school. The guidance counsellor was contacted, and then my parents. Everyone was worried. And with no other option, my parents brought me back to the emergency room.

I felt drained—physically and emotionally. In my mind, I kept thinking, *No one can help me unless they let me die.* The hospital felt cold and impersonal. We waited for hours before a psychiatrist finally came to see me.

While we sat in that waiting room, I told myself that no one cared—not even my parents. They barely said a word to me. But looking back, I think they were just trying not to say the wrong thing. They were scared, too.

Eventually, the psychiatrist arrived and sat across from me. After my parents stepped out to give us privacy, the first thing he said was, "Why did you write a suicide note?" No introduction. No warmth. I stared at him. *You want me to open up to a complete stranger, and you can't even ask me how I'm doing?*

"You don't know what happened to me," I said sharply. "You have no idea why I feel this way. And you're not going to find out. I just want to go home."

"I don't feel comfortable sending you home," he replied. He couldn't release me. Instead, he recommended I be transferred to a crisis stabilization unit—CSU. I had already told them I didn't want to go back to the psych ward, and this was the alternative.

There wasn't much choice. The mobile crisis team was called in to take me. I waited another hour in the emergency room until they arrived. When they finally did, I thought maybe—just maybe—I could talk my way out of this. Convince them I was fine. Safe. But deep down, I knew better. My parents wanted me home, but they were scared too. And the psychiatrist had already made the decision. I wasn't going home that night.

The two staff members from the mobile crisis team sat with me, trying to start a conversation. I stared at the floor, saying the same thing over and over. "I'm fine. I can go home." But I think they knew I wasn't. Eventually, I was told to gather my things. We walked out together to the parking lot. My parents followed us to the car. When I realized they couldn't come with me, my heart sank. I had to say goodbye right there in the parking lot. I watched them drive away, and I saw my mom crying in the front seat.

It was a twenty-minute drive to the CSU. I sat in the very back of the car, silent, staring out the window. The sky was black, the air cold, the headlights from other cars blurring past. They all looked like they had somewhere to go. And in that moment, I wished I was in any car but the one I was in. The drive was silent—until the driver looked at me through the rearview mirror.

"What gives you the feeling that you need to end your life?" he asked. "You're blessed with two parents who love you and are doing everything they can to support you." His words hit me hard. I wanted to scream.

"You don't know what my life is like," I snapped. "Just because I have supportive parents doesn't mean everything's been easy. You have no idea what I've been through." After that, there was silence again. I kept my head down the rest of the way, staring at my feet, feeling the weight of everything I couldn't say.

When we arrived, I was told, "Wait here—we'll open the door for you." I glanced up at the building. It looked unfamiliar and intimidating. My first instinct was to run. But the moment I stepped out, I was calmly told, "Stay with us."

I kept my head low as we walked inside. The doors buzzed shut behind me, locking automatically. A lump formed in my throat. It felt like I was stepping into something unknown—but what I didn't realize was that this place would end up being part of what helped save me.

The CSU looked nothing like the psych ward I'd expected. It felt less like a hospital and more like a home. There was a common area that looked like a living room, with couches and a TV. A kitchen nearby. Staff offices. A sensory room. And a hallway with smaller rooms—one of which would be mine.

I had to walk up so many stairs just to get there. Every step felt heavier than the last—not because of the climb, but because of everything I was carrying inside. When we finally reached the top, a staff member opened the door and let us in. I kept my head down as we stepped inside. Then I heard it—the door buzzing shut behind us, locking automatically. A lump rose in my throat. I didn't know what I was walking into, and part of me didn't want to find out.

But then, someone met me with warmth. A staff member with a gentle voice introduced herself as Rebecca. She didn't seem rushed or cold—just calm. She led me into a small intake room where a round table waited in the center. I sat down with her and the Mobile Crisis team, my body still tense, unsure.

Rebecca looked at me kindly and asked if I wanted to explain why I was there, or if I'd rather let the Mobile Crisis team speak. I couldn't find the words. I looked at them, silently asking for help. They understood—and they stepped in, explaining what had happened and why I needed support.

When they finished, one of them looked at me softly. "I hope you take care of yourself, Kaylynne," they said with quiet sincerity.

Then, with a nod to Rebecca, they stood and left the room. The door clicked shut behind them, and suddenly it was just the two of us.

Rebecca turned toward me with that same steady calmness. She began filling out paperwork, occasionally looking up to ask brief questions—never pushing, just checking in. Her presence wasn't cold, but she didn't sugarcoat anything either. Just clear, professional, and calm.

Then came the question I'd been bracing for.

"Do you still have thoughts of harming yourself?"

My chest tightened. I didn't want to admit anything. I was still drowning inside, but I couldn't bring myself to say the words.

So I lied.

"I'm okay. I feel safe now."

Maybe she believed me. Maybe she didn't.

But she didn't challenge it.

She just nodded, wrote something down, and let the silence speak for what I couldn't.

Once the paperwork was done, she let me know she needed to go through my belongings. She carefully searched my bag, checking each item. Then she explained I could either change into their clothing or keep wearing my own if I was okay with her removing the strings. I chose to keep mine, so she took a pair of scissors and gently cut the strings from my hoodie and pants.

Then she showed me around the unit.

The CSU didn't feel like a psych ward at all. It was one big, open space that felt calm and lived in—more like a place to rest than a place to be watched. Right when you walked in, the staff offices were to the side, open and visible but not intimidating. In the center was a common area with couches and a TV, where people could sit together without pressure. A cozy sensory room was tucked quietly into the corner, offering a soft space to breathe. Along the outer walls were six small bedrooms, each with real bedding—thick comforters, soft pillows, and none of the stiff, paper-thin blankets I remembered from the psych ward. There was a private space to shower or bathe, stocked with actual shampoo, conditioner, and body wash—not the generic hospital kind. It wasn't perfect, but it felt safe. And right then, that was more than enough.

Eventually, I was brought to my room. The second I was alone, I broke down. I cried until I fell asleep. I must have been completely drained, because when I opened my eyes again, it was morning.

There was a knock at the door. A new staff member stepped in with a small cup of meds. "Hey, I'm Megan," she said softly. "I'm just here to give you these." I nodded and took the cup from her hands, swallowing the pills without saying much. She didn't rush out. Instead, she stayed for a moment. "Just so you know," she added gently, "I'm here if you ever want to talk. Anytime. You're not alone." She started to leave, then paused at the doorway. "How are you doing today?" she asked—like she actually cared what the answer was.

I didn't have the strength to lie. "I just can't do it anymore," I whispered. "I've been feeling like this for so long. All I want is to leave." She stepped inside, left the door cracked, and sat on the edge of the bed. She looked at me like she actually saw me.

"I know how exhausting it is to fight a war no one else can see," she said. "When your own mind becomes the enemy, it's easy to think this is how it will always be. But I want you to hear me—this doesn't have to be forever."

I didn't say anything, but I was listening. "You have a choice," she said. "Even if it's just a tiny one at first. You can stay in the darkness, or you can choose—little by little—to start climbing out."

Those words stayed with me. Not right away. I didn't believe her in the moment. But something in me needed to hear that. That I had a choice.

Before she left, she added one more thing. "You don't always have to fight your battles alone. Asking for help doesn't make you weak—it means you're still trying. And that matters."

That conversation didn't magically fix everything. But it cracked something open. For a moment, I felt like someone actually saw through the silence. A few days later, I was discharged from the CSU. I was still drowning in everything I didn't know how to say—but that small moment with Megan stayed with me. It didn't save me. But it reminded me that maybe, just maybe, I was worth saving.

CHAPTER 8

I Give Up

Back in eighth grade, a speaker came to our school to talk about suicide. I remember him saying that around 800,000 people take their own lives every year—that's one person every forty seconds. I couldn't believe how many people wanted to end their lives. At the time, it felt distant. Tragic, but not personal.

Now I understand. For some people, suicide feels like drowning. For me, it was like trying to push a massive boulder uphill—one that wouldn't budge no matter how hard I tried. That's what my life felt like after the rape. Every day, every hour, I was battling thoughts I couldn't silence. It was exhausting just to survive. But there was one thing the speaker said that stuck with me: *"There are too many people who die by suicide each year, which means there are too many people who lost a fight they could have won."*

At the time, I believed him. But now? After what I'd been through? It didn't feel like a fight I could win. Every moment felt like death was hovering over me. I spent my days trying to silence the demons in my head and my nights trying to hide from them. I didn't just want the pain to stop—I wanted to disappear. The thought of taking my own life terrified me... but not as much as the thought of continuing to live like this.

At some point, I stopped believing that anyone could save me. I felt completely alone. The truth? Maybe the only person who could save me was myself—but I didn't know how. I didn't even know if surviving this was possible. Three months had passed since the rape, and school had become unbearable. Noah was everywhere—his face, his voice, his presence haunted the hallways. Every time I saw him, the pain came back all over again.

After my time in the psych ward and CSU, my parents had become more open to letting me stay home. I was grateful. But sometimes, they'd suddenly switch—reminding me I needed an education, forcing me out the door whether I was ready or not.

And the school itself wasn't any better. Some of my teachers were more annoyed than supportive. A few even told me I might never graduate. "I can see you being a high school dropout," one said.

What they didn't know was that I didn't expect to live long enough to graduate anyway. On the days I did make it to school, I could see the relief on my parents' faces. Just watching me walk out the front door made them happy. But what they didn't realize was that most of the time, I was still dying inside.

Tuesdays, Wednesdays, and Thursdays were different. I woke up with a small spark of something—because those were Taekwondo days. Even when I didn't have the motivation to face school, I still looked forward to training. It was the only thing that kept me moving forward. As I walked into the dojang, I took in the familiar sights and sounds: the shuffle of feet, the sharp snap of kicks, the rhythm of bodies pushing their limits. The energy in the room was something I could feel deep in my chest—focused, powerful, alive.

Before class, I followed my routine. Deep breath. Positive self-talk. Tighten my belt. No matter what chaos was happening inside me, I tried to keep it together. Taekwondo was more than just a sport—it was my fire. It gave me purpose. It reminded me of who I used to be and who I still wanted to become. With every strike against the bag, I felt a rush of relief. But even in that moment of release, a darker thought crept in: *I wish I could unleash this power on him.*

Taekwondo had always been my safe space—a second home filled with people who felt more like family than teammates. But even there, I started pulling away. I tugged my sleeves down every time I punched, hiding the scars on my arms. I avoided eye contact, afraid that if anyone really looked at me, they'd see just how broken I was. The fear of judgment started to outweigh the comfort I once felt. I began questioning if I even belonged anymore.

But then I remembered something my master instructor had told me over a year earlier: *"You can talk to me about anything."* Something in me shifted. After class one day, I waited until the room had cleared, then walked up to her. I told her what I'd been doing to my body. I expected disappointment. Shame. Maybe even anger. But what I got instead was compassion. She listened. Without judgment. Without trying to fix me. Just listened. And for the first time in a long time, I felt like I could breathe.

But even knowing there were people who cared—it still didn't feel like enough. Because no one could reach into the place where I was trapped. No one could save me from the pain I carried alone. December 27 was coming. And I had already made up my mind. I sat down at my desk, the faint sound of Christmas music still echoing in the background. But it didn't bring joy—only heaviness. I picked up a pen, my hand trembling, and began to write what I believed would be the final words my family would ever hear from me.

December 27. I told myself it would be the last day I'd ever have to feel anything. This time, I didn't just write goodbye. I wrote the truth.

> I understand that you are sad, but please think about how happy I am. Believe me when I say choosing this path was the best option. Try to see it as a way to set me free—from pain, from the past,

from the memories you don't know Memories of the countless times I was raped and assaulted by Noah. I've never stopped loving you.

I'm sorry I didn't have the strength to keep fighting so we could stay together. Please take care of each other.

Love always,

Kaylynne xoxo

That night, I went to bed believing it would be my last. I told my dad I loved him before he left for work—knowing it would be the final time. Later that morning, I sat on my bed crying. The next moments blurred together. Pills. Blood. Silence. Then—regret.

A switch flipped in my head. *I shouldn't have done this.* I felt lightheaded and nauseous. I stared at the blood running down my arms. I tried to undo it—to purge what I had taken—but it was too late. My mom heard me from the hallway and came into the room. Her eyes darted between me, the blood, and the note on my desk.

"What did you take?" she asked, panic rising in her voice.

"I'm okay," I lied.

"You're clearly not okay. What did you take?"

Tears filled my eyes. "I took something I shouldn't have. I'm sorry."

My mom called my dad, who told her to call 911. I heard the panic in her voice when she made the call. It was the first time in my life I had ever seen my mom cry like that. The fear in her eyes—real, raw—filled me with a regret deeper than I knew was possible.

The last time I'd been in an ambulance, I was on a preschool field trip to the fire station. Now, I was strapped to a stretcher, feeling like I was falling apart.

I looked at the paramedic next to me and noticed a piece of paper in his jacket pocket. "What's that?" I asked nervously.

"It's your suicide note. I'm going to give it to the doctors so they can better understand what's going on."

"No. Please don't do that." If I was still alive, that letter wasn't supposed to be seen. It wasn't meant for anyone unless I was gone. I instantly regretted leaving it on my desk so visibly.

When we arrived at the hospital, I wasn't prepared for what I saw—my grandparents. My heart sank. Their eyes locked on mine as I was wheeled in on the stretcher, and I wanted to disappear. The shame was unbearable. It was already hard enough facing my parents. Now, my grandparents knew too.

My mom, sensing my discomfort, quietly told them to leave. They did. Later, I learned that my dad had asked them to meet us there because he had to be at work. It wasn't his fault—but the humiliation still clung to me.

Lying in the emergency room, I kept wondering if the paramedic had handed over my note. If anyone had read it. If they knew what I'd been through. I hoped they hadn't.

Now that I was alive, I didn't want those words to exist anymore. I felt torn. One part of me was relieved that I'd survived. The other part wished I hadn't—because facing what came next felt impossible. After seven days in the psych ward, the doctors said I was stable enough to go home.

That's when I was officially diagnosed with anxiety—on top of the depression they had already identified earlier. The hospital was becoming too familiar—something I never wanted, but somehow expected.

When I returned to school, no one asked questions. No one wondered where I'd been. That didn't bother me. I had no plans to tell them. Being back around so many people felt strange—overwhelming, even—but when I thought back to the psych ward, there was something about it that had felt safer. He didn't know where I was then. He couldn't reach me. He couldn't hurt me.

But the moment I stepped back into the real world, that safety was gone. The memories followed me everywhere. And sometimes, I couldn't help but think… maybe it would've been easier if he had just killed me the first time he raped me. Because living with the aftermath felt harder than dying ever could. And even though I had survived, deep down, I knew the idea of ending my life hadn't fully left me—not yet.

CHAPTER 9

Stuck In My Mind

After seven days in the psych ward, nothing had really changed. If anything, my thoughts about death had only gotten worse. My self-harm had escalated. I wasn't expecting a miracle—but some part of me had hoped for a shift, a sign, anything. Instead, I felt more hopeless than ever.

I tried to end my life again while I was there—in the bathroom—but no one ever found out. I didn't go through with it completely. It wasn't that I wanted to die entirely. What I really wanted was for a part of me to disappear—the broken part, the violated part. I didn't want to live with her anymore.

I barely spoke to anyone on the unit. I stayed in my nearly empty room, locked inside myself. I did talk to my parents during their visits—they came almost every day. But even with the psychiatrist I saw each morning, I couldn't say anything real. All I ever told him was, "I want to go home."

When I finally did return home, I wasn't the same. I kept to myself most of the time, but I also started lashing out—yelling, snapping, exploding over the smallest things. My family didn't know what was happening to me. How could they? The trauma in my head had found a way to leak out into everything else.

Even with everything spiralling, I had moments—brief, brave moments—when I wanted to speak up. Sometimes I'd walk up to my mom with the intention of telling her the truth about what Noah did to me. I'd open my mouth, ready to say it... but nothing would come out.

I'd stare at the floor and whisper, "I have something important to tell you."

She'd gently ask, "What is it?"

And I'd panic, mumble, "Never mind," and walk away.

It happened over and over. I spent most of my time alone in my room, buried under blankets that felt like the only safe place left in the world. I didn't feel like I was living inside my body. It was like I was renting it—and I hated every inch of it. I didn't want to be here anymore. I didn't want to be *me* anymore.

Under those covers, I felt like a child again, hiding from monsters under the bed. But this time, the monster lived inside my own head. It whispered things to me I didn't know how to silence.

Everything became too much—school, therapy, pretending. But Taekwondo... that was still my one thing. My reason. My outlet. The one part of my life that gave me any sense of purpose.

School no longer felt like a priority—not because I didn't care, but because it didn't feel safe. Taekwondo came first. It had to. Noah had stolen my sense of safety in every hallway, every classroom. And somehow, that had stolen my motivation, too.

Another teacher—different from the one who'd said it before— told me he thought I'd become a high school dropout. I didn't argue. Secretly, I believed it.

My mind was exhausted. I kept wishing there was a reset button—something to bring me back to the person I used to be. The girl without scars. Without suicidal thoughts. Without the memory of being held down and broken. But there was no reset button. Just me. And the present. A present that felt completely out of control.

The more I tried to stay grounded, the more my memories pulled me under. I had good ones—my family, some of my Taekwondo accomplishments—but they were drowned out by the worst experiences of my life. My brain was like a broken radio, stuck on a station that only played the same horror scene on repeat.

After being discharged, I started therapy once a week. I was still under the care of a psychiatrist from my time in the psych ward, but it didn't feel like she was helping. To be fair, I wasn't really talking. I was too scared to tell the truth. I was convinced that if I told someone I'd been raped, they wouldn't believe me—or worse, they'd treat me like it didn't matter. Just like the resource teacher. Just like the guidance counsellor.

So our sessions were mostly silence. She'd ask questions. I'd stare at the floor. The only thing I really noticed was how cluttered her desk and bookshelves were—papers stacked, books leaning sideways. The mess made me feel like I couldn't breathe. Like everything around me was just as overwhelming as the chaos in my head. The only good thing about therapy was that it meant missing school. Even if it was just for an hour, it gave me a break from that building—and from him.

But outside of those sessions, I kept sinking. There was a small part of me that wanted help, but I didn't know how to ask. I started to notice something, though—something that stuck with me: When I acted like I was okay, nobody seemed worried. But when I hurt myself, people started paying attention. It started to feel like I had to be in crisis just to be taken seriously. If I wanted help, I had to prove I was breaking. And that belief grew stronger with every passing day.

I carried a blade with me everywhere I went. For me, it wasn't just an object—it was a form of control. A lifeline. I knew that if the pain in my chest became too much, I had a way to release it. A way to survive it.

Most days, I didn't even make it to class. I wandered the halls, trying to stay invisible. But Noah always found me. He'd pull me to the back of the school and take me outside. It was like some sick game of hide and seek—only I was the one hiding, and he always won. I was tired. I was scared. And I was numb.

I'd beg him to stop, but it was never enough. Afterward, I would retreat to the washroom and hurt myself. Cutting became my way of escaping the trauma he left behind. But one day, I cut too deep. I needed stitches.

I remember thinking, *This was a mistake.* Not because I regretted the pain—but because the weekend was my Taekwondo tournament. And now, I couldn't compete.

I was devastated. Taekwondo was the only thing that made me feel alive. The pounding of my heart before stepping onto the mat—the mix of nerves and excitement—that was the only time I could breathe. The only time I felt like I had control. My parents thought the stitches would be a wake-up call. That hurting myself like that—enough to need medical care—would finally make me stop. But it didn't.

Instead, my body became a canvas. Cut after cut. Scar after scar. I couldn't stop. Each mark was like a message I couldn't say out loud. A scream no one could hear. Those scars would stay with me forever. Every time I looked in the mirror, I felt like I was staring through broken glass. I could see the girl I used to be—just barely—but she looked like a ghost now.

A version of me frozen in time, tears in her eyes, silently begging to go back to before. Back to when everything still made sense. Before the psych ward. Before the hospital. Before him.

I stopped caring about my body. I stopped respecting what I had. Depression ran so deep that I couldn't even pretend to love myself anymore. My parents tried. They really did. They checked in. They stayed close. They offered love over and over again.

But for some reason, it still wasn't enough.

CHAPTER 10

Trying To Help Myself

My 15th birthday came and went, but as I blew out the candles on my cake, one thought kept echoing in my mind: *I hope I'm not here to blow out the candles on my 16th.*

My behaviour had gotten worse. I was self-harming more often. My parents were growing more and more concerned, but I didn't know how to give them answers I didn't have. Two days after my birthday, on February 12, 2019, I went to therapy. I don't know what made me say it, but I told my psychiatrist how low I'd been feeling—and how often I'd been having urges to hurt myself.

She looked at me and gently asked, "Have you been using any positive coping skills?" I told her no. The only thing that had helped me survive up to that point was self-harm. She asked me to try thinking of just one healthy coping mechanism—just one thing that had ever made me feel better. I'd been asked that before, but this time, something was different. This time, I sat with the question. And then it came to me: *Taekwondo.*

I don't remember everything else we talked about that day, but something about that session made me want to try. Really try. For the first time in a long time, I wanted to change. When I got home,

I started thinking about what it would take to escape the cycle I was stuck in—hospital visits, self-harm, suicide attempts. I didn't know where to start. But I wanted to try.

That night, while lying in bed and staring at the ceiling, a different voice crept into my thoughts: *You'll never change.* And for a second, I believed it. Then my phone buzzed. It was a message from Jessica, a friend from school I hadn't talked to in a while.

"Kaylynne, I know we haven't been talking much, but I want you to know I'm here for you. You're stronger than you think. I hope everything's okay. I'm always here if you want to talk."

I didn't reply. I couldn't. But it meant more than she'll ever know. Just knowing that someone cared enough to check in—that someone believed I had strength even when I didn't—shifted something in me. I didn't feel strong, but maybe I could pretend for now. Maybe that was enough.

So I started to fight again. For the version of me that used to love life. For the girl who loved training. I pushed myself to work out at home. I went to the gym. I focused on getting stronger. For a little while, it worked. Taekwondo helped me feel like I was finding myself again. But looking back, I see it clearly now—I was still carrying a secret that was too heavy to hold alone. And I was trying to rebuild my life without letting go of the thing that was crushing me.

My family was proud of me. They saw me going to the gym, training at home, eating healthy again—like I was finally becoming myself. And for a while, I believed it too. I poured everything I had into Taekwondo. I was training harder than ever before, and my results showed it. I started winning gold medals, tournament after tournament. Every match felt like a war, and every win felt like I was clawing a little bit of myself back.

In March 2019, I earned gold in sparring and silver in patterns. My hard work wasn't just paying off—it was speaking for itself. Then came one of the biggest challenges of all: a two-day high-performance training camp in Moose Jaw, Saskatchewan. It was a seven-hour drive from home, and even just getting there felt like a milestone. The first day was three hours long. The second was eight hours of nonstop drills, conditioning, and sparring.

It pushed me past what I thought I was capable of. My legs were sore. My body screamed for rest. But I didn't quit. I gave everything I had to that mat. When it ended, I felt something rare—something I hadn't felt in what felt like forever:

Pride.

Happiness.

Accomplishment.

I'd earned it. And for a moment, I believed maybe I was getting better. But even in that moment, I could feel the weight creeping back in. The part of me that still hadn't spoken the truth. The part that was still carrying guilt for freezing. For not fighting back. For not being able to remember how.

Every time I saw someone online say, *"If it were me, I would've fought back,"* it gutted me. Because I didn't. And I hated myself for it. Even as I stood on the podium, gold medal around my neck, part of me still felt like a failure.

As 2019 went on, most people assumed I was doing well. I kept bringing home medals. I stayed focused on training. I smiled in photos. On May 26th, I was awarded a trophy for being the top female competitor. Not long after, I was even featured on the news as the sports star of the week.

To the outside world, I looked unstoppable. But inside, I was still breaking. I had gotten really good at masking. I knew how to act like I was okay, even when I wasn't. I knew how to show up, train hard, and smile through it all—even while carrying pain that no one could see. Taekwondo gave me something to hold onto. Something to believe in. I used training as my way of coping. And for a time, it worked.

But I hadn't told anyone the truth. I hadn't spoken about the trauma. I hadn't let go of the guilt. And that silence was slowly drowning me. By April, the weight of everything I had buried caught up with me. I attempted to take my life again.

Same routine: the hospital, then the psych ward. Another cycle. Another silence. Another scar. I was exhausted—mentally, physically, emotionally. I had poured everything I had into getting better. I had done the work, pushed my body, chased medals, smiled through pain.

But none of it had been enough. And deep down, I was starting to believe that maybe nothing ever would be.

CHAPTER 11

Living In A Mental Health Crisis

By the time summer came, I had stopped believing I could help myself. But I still kept going to Taekwondo—somehow. It was the only thread of normalcy I had left. High school felt like a battlefield. I only earned one credit—Grade 9 science. The rest was a blur of missed classes, panic, and trauma.

I'd lost count of how many times I was assaulted at school. Lost track of how many times he knocked on my door just to touch me.

Giving up on myself didn't happen all at once. It was slow, silent, and dangerous. I felt like I was always teetering on the edge of crisis. Like I was being swallowed whole by something I couldn't stop.

And when the pressure got too much—when I couldn't contain the chaos in my chest—I started running. From home. From school. From everything.

One night, it all got too loud inside my head. I bolted from the house without thinking and ended up in a nearby park. I sat there, knees pulled to my chest, crying. Wishing I could forget. Wishing I could just stop feeling altogether. I didn't want to die—I just didn't want to be this version of myself anymore. I felt like a lost cause.

I sat on a wooden bench, numb and shaking, with no idea what to do next. Then my phone buzzed. Again and again. It was my mom.

Mom, 6:15 p.m.: *Call me… Dad's been trying to get ahold of you.*

Me, 6:20 p.m.: *LEAVE ME ALONE.*

Mom, 6:22 p.m.: *Okay… Just please don't be long.*

Mom, 7:43 p.m.: *Call me or text me.*

Mom, 7:47 p.m.: *Are you doing okay?*

Mom, 7:50 p.m.: *We need to know if you're okay.*

Mom, 8:27 p.m.: *Come home, Kay. We're worried about you.*

Me, 8:30 p.m.: *No. I'm not coming home.*

Mom, 8:31 p.m.: *Please. Dad and I are really worried.*

Me, 8:33 p.m.: *You don't hear me. I'm not coming home. I can't do this anymore. I just want to end it.*

Mom, 8:34 p.m.: *Please come home. We love you.*

Mom, 8:57 p.m.: *I can pick you up.*

Mom, 9:02 p.m.: *I know you're feeling helpless. It breaks my heart. Can I please come and get you?*

Mom, 9:08 p.m.: *If you're not home in 10 minutes, we'll have to call the police. You have to answer your phone.*

I read her messages again and again. I didn't feel ready to go back, but those words—*You have to go back home*—looped through my mind. I wiped the tears from my face and stood up. My legs felt like they belonged to someone else. But somehow, I walked.

When I got home, my parents were waiting. They didn't yell. They didn't panic. They just looked at me like they didn't know how to help anymore. My mom asked why I ran. I said nothing. I wished they already knew. I wished someone did. I felt broken. Like all the pieces of me had shattered and no one could put them back together. I had cuts on my arms. Scars no one understood. And now, hallucinations.

I started seeing him everywhere—on the street, in my room, in shadows that weren't real. I'd wake up believing he was standing over me. Sometimes, I thought I heard his voice. I didn't know what was real anymore. And worse, I didn't know how to tell anyone. The hallucinations weren't just occasional—they were constant.

Every day, I felt like I was slipping further from reality. I'd flinch at shadows. Freeze at familiar shapes. Sometimes I swore I saw him in the corner of my room or walking just a few steps behind me. I'd turn around—and nothing would be there. But the fear stayed. The image stayed. And no one else could see what I was seeing.

It made me question everything.

Had I lost my mind?

Was this what broken looked like?

Was this who I was now?

I didn't know how to explain it to anyone. I was terrified of what people would think—terrified that if I told the truth, I'd be dismissed, laughed at, or locked away. So I stayed quiet. And in that silence, my fear grew louder. My pain sharpened. I started attempting suicide more often—desperate for an escape from a mind that wouldn't give me peace.

More trips to the emergency room followed. I didn't go because I wanted help. I went because I didn't know what else to do. I didn't know how to survive in a world that felt like it was chasing me— even when I was alone.

CHAPTER 12

Turning Point

By late 2019, I was assigned a new therapist. I'm still not sure why the change happened, but I walked into those sessions hoping he could help pull me out of the storm I was drowning in. I told him what I'd been too afraid to say out loud: that I was seeing... someone. Or something.

It had a shape I recognized. A presence that felt like him. Sometimes, I swore I could feel it behind me—on sidewalks, in classrooms, even while walking home. When I told people, they'd say, "There's no one there." But to me, he was everywhere. I needed help.

But instead of exploring what I meant, the therapist brushed it off. "You're not schizophrenic," he said, shifting the conversation back to my depression. He didn't offer tools or coping strategies. I started to believe I wasn't fixable. I thought someone had to save me—that someone else needed to rescue me from drowning.

What I didn't know yet was that I would have to learn how to swim myself. I tried to keep functioning—going to school, going to therapy, pretending everything was fine. But I was unravelling.

And then came November 14th, 2019. It began with thirteen missed calls from Noah. I didn't want to answer. But on the thirteenth try, I picked up. "What do you want?" I asked, my voice low, guarded.

"You better be at school tomorrow," he said. "If I don't see you at your locker, I'll come to your house. With a knife."

That was all he said before the line went dead. I was paralyzed. I kept hearing his voice over and over again in my head. Be at your locker if you want to stay alive.

I didn't sleep that night. The next morning, I begged my parents not to make me go to school. I told them I wasn't feeling well, that something didn't feel right. But they didn't know what I was really trying to say—*that I was terrified.*

We ended up getting into an argument. I don't remember all the words that were said—just yelling, frustration, and panic building in my chest.

Eventually, I gave in and decided to go. I told myself maybe it was better than waiting at home, wondering if he'd show up. At least if I was at school, I'd see it coming. When I walked through those school doors, every step felt heavy. I skipped my locker and went straight to the resource room. That had become my safe zone, even if it didn't feel safe anymore. I sat down and tried to stay invisible.

That's when I overheard a conversation. A teacher told one of the EAs that Noah had apparently dropped out of school. My heart raced. *If he dropped out... Why did he call me? Why threaten me to come to school?*

The bell rang. I was still seated when the resource teacher turned to me and said, "You need to get to class now. It's already November and you haven't completed a single assignment. If you keep this up, you won't graduate on time."

"I know," I whispered.

"Last year, you only passed one class," she added, pushing harder.

I sighed. "Okay. I'll go." I grabbed my things and walked—slowly, carefully—toward my locker. He was there. He was leaning against the locker like he hadn't destroyed my entire life. Like nothing had happened. Like we were still just two teenagers who used to talk at lunch.

"Hey," he said, smirking. "Wasn't sure if you'd actually show up. Thought maybe I'd have to swing by your place since you didn't answer me yesterday." My stomach dropped. He had hung up on me. He was the one who ended the call after threatening me—but here he was, acting like *I* was the one avoiding him.

"I'm not going to that stupid school anymore," he added. "Dropped out. But don't think that means I'm not gonna see you. I still will." Then his voice dropped lower. "Anyway… you know why I'm here." He stepped forward, and I turned and ran.

I locked myself in a bathroom stall and collapsed. I couldn't breathe. I looked at the blade in my hand, thinking maybe this was it. But something inside me shifted—I wasn't sure if I wanted to die, or if I just didn't know how to live like this anymore.

For the first time, something shifted. My phone was buried in my bag. I pulled it out, my hands shaking, and stared at the screen. I didn't know what to say. I didn't even know if I wanted help. But somehow, I found the number for the mobile crisis team and hit call. A woman answered.

Her voice was calm and warm, but I barely got the words out. "I don't feel safe… not with myself," I said. "And I can't keep doing this. I have a plan." She asked me some questions—gently—and listened without judgment.

At the end of the call, she said, "Kaylynne, based on what you've told me, I think it's safest if you come to the Crisis Stabilization Unit. We'll arrange for someone to pick you up." I said yes. Because as much as I didn't want to be locked away again… I didn't want to die either.

I ended the call and sat frozen in the bathroom stall, still gripping the phone like it was the only thing holding me together. I didn't know what I had just agreed to. I only knew I didn't want to see him again. I couldn't risk him finding me at school.

When I finally felt steady enough, I peeked out from the stall, heart racing. The hallway was quiet when I slipped out of the bathroom. I walked fast—not quite running, but close—straight to the front doors and out of the school. Once I was outside, I called my mom.

My voice cracked as soon as she picked up. "I'm sorry," I said through tears. "I can't do this anymore. I called the mobile crisis team… and I'm going to the CSU."

There was a pause. I don't remember her exact words—I just remember the heaviness in her voice, like she didn't know whether to cry or hold it together for me. "Okay," she said gently. "Come home. I'll wait with you."

When I got home, I went straight to my room and closed the door behind me. I didn't want to face anyone—not my mom, not my dad, not even myself. I sat on the floor with my back pressed against the door, knees pulled up to my chest. My mom knocked gently, trying to talk to me through the door, her voice shaky and full of concern. But I couldn't respond. I didn't have the words, and I didn't have the strength.

"Please," she said quietly. "I love you. Me and Dad—we're here for you. We're just really scared." I stayed silent. Half an hour later, I heard another knock—the one that wasn't hers.

The mobile crisis team had arrived. My mom let them in and told them I was in my room. I heard their voices as they came down the hallway, soft but serious.

Then came another knock, followed by, "Hey, Kaylynne. It's us, the mobile crisis team. Can we come in and talk?" I didn't answer. "We're going to open the door slowly, okay?" one of them said. "We just want to make sure you're safe."

They stepped into the room slowly, keeping their distance but speaking with calm, familiar voices. "Hey, Kaylynne," one of them said. "We know things have been really hard lately. We're worried about you. Would you be willing to come with us to the CSU for a little while?"

I nodded without saying a word. "Do you want to grab a few things before we go?" one of them asked.

"No," I muttered. "I don't need anything."

That's when my mom stepped closer. "Are you sure?" she asked softly. "That's not like you... not to bring anything."

But I didn't care. I didn't even look at her. "Goodbye," I said under my breath.

She tried to hold it together, but I could hear the shake in her voice as she whispered, "I love you."

Without a bag, without a jacket, without anything at all, I walked out the door with the mobile crisis team—quiet, numb, and completely empty. When I arrived at the Crisis Stabilization Unit, I was met with familiar faces. The staff remembered me—not with judgment or pity, but with quiet understanding.

There was something about the way they greeted me that made it feel like I wasn't just another crisis. I was a person. A person in pain.

They gave me a room. A safe space. A fresh chance to breathe. It didn't feel like punishment. It felt like someone finally saw how much I was hurting—and didn't turn away. Then the hallucinations came back—sharper, stronger. He was everywhere. In the corners. In the shadows. In the echoes of footsteps that didn't belong to anyone. I locked myself in my room and spiralled. The fear was unbearable, like being hunted by someone no one else could see.

The staff responded quickly. They moved with urgency and care, removing anything I could use to hurt myself. One of them, clearly overwhelmed, said something that stung: "You're influencing the others."

That was never my intention. I was just in a crisis. Eventually, they called my mom. They told her they thought it was best for me to go to the hospital—and that she should be the one to bring me there.

When my mom arrived, I was still in my room. The plan was for her to take me, but the second the doors opened and I saw my chance, I ran. I bolted before anyone could stop me.

My mom chased after me. She drove around, trying to find me. But I didn't stop running. I was desperate to get away, to disappear.

Eventually, a police car pulled up behind me. I didn't stop when they told me to. So they ran after me. Tackled me. Cuffed me. Dragged me into the back of their cruiser as I screamed, "I just want to die!" At the ER, I was placed under constant watch—security guards monitoring my every move.

After what felt like hours, a nurse finally came and said the words I was dreading: "We're moving you to the psych ward."

I panicked. I tried to run. I tried to fight. But they held me down. They brought me into a cold, empty room. Just a bare mattress on the floor, a scratchy anti-suicide blanket, and a camera mounted in the corner. No pillow. No privacy. Just fluorescent lights and the quiet threat of what was coming.

A group of staff entered—nurses and security guards. One of them said calmly, "We need to remove your clothes for safety." But something inside me snapped. I started screaming. Kicking. Fighting.

Before I could fully process what was happening, the security guards grabbed me and threw me down onto the mattress. My back hit the floor hard. I thrashed, terrified, as they held me down.

"Please stop!" I cried. "Don't touch me!" But they didn't stop. They couldn't. Not until it was done. Pinned to the mattress by multiple guards, I felt the cold bite of trauma shears as the nurses began cutting off my clothes. It didn't matter that this was for safety. In that moment, my mind couldn't separate the past from the present. I wasn't in a hospital—I was back in the place where everything first went wrong.

I begged them to stop. But the more I screamed, the more it all blurred together. And then it was over. They handed me a heavy, stiff blanket and a gown made from the same thick material—designed so I couldn't hurt myself. It was scratchy and uncomfortable, but safety came before comfort.

The door locked behind them. I was alone—just me, the walls, and the silent, watching eye of the camera. That night felt endless. I didn't sleep. I couldn't. Every second dragged like a lifetime.

But the next morning, a nurse came to the door and said, "We've got a regular room for you now." It was a relief I didn't expect. They brought me out of seclusion and into a normal room on the ward. A bed that was actually comfortable to sleep on. A door that didn't feel like a prison. I still had to wear the safety gown and use the anti-suicide blanket—but at least I wasn't locked away alone anymore. It still didn't feel safe in my mind, but the space felt a little more human.

Ten days later, I was granted a weekend pass. But when I lashed out again at home, I was brought back. This time, the team started talking about placing me somewhere long-term. Somewhere outside my home. Somewhere I didn't want to go. That terrified me.

One night, I sat alone in the ward lounge, staring out the window like it might offer answers. The glass was foggy from the inside, the lights of passing cars outside nothing more than blurred streaks. I wasn't looking for anything specific. I just didn't want to go back to my room.

Then someone sat beside me. She didn't say anything at first. Just pulled her legs up onto the chair and sat with her arms wrapped around them. We sat in silence for a while—both of us too tired to fill the space with anything fake. "It sucks in here, doesn't it?" she finally said, not looking at me.

"Yeah," I said quietly.

She glanced over, studying me like she already knew I wasn't okay. "You don't talk much, do you?"

I shrugged. "I guess I don't really have anything to say."

She just nodded a little and said, "I'm Abby."

"Kaylynne."

We both looked forward again. It was quiet for a while. Then I don't know why I said it—but I gave her a small piece of the truth. "Sometimes… I think there's something wrong with me."

She looked over again. "What do you mean?"

I shook my head. "Never mind."

But she kept her eyes on me, gentle but steady. "You don't have to tell me. But… I've been there. Feeling like you're broken. Like you're carrying something so heavy it's easier to pretend it's not even there." I didn't respond, but I felt it. Like she could see the parts of me I hadn't shown anyone.

And then she said it—not bluntly, not dramatically—just quietly. Like it was something she had said before, and still found hard to say. "I didn't tell anyone what happened to me for three years. I was raped… and I thought staying quiet would keep me safe.

But the silence? It almost destroyed me." I turned toward her slowly, not sure how to react. My heart was pounding. I hadn't said it out loud—not to anyone. But somehow, she knew. Somehow, she saw the shadow I was carrying. She didn't push me. She didn't ask for details. She just said, "You don't have to tell me anything. I just want you to know you're not the only one."

I opened my mouth to speak, but the words caught in my throat. "Something happened to me too," I whispered. "But… I can't say it. Not yet."

Abby nodded like she understood completely. "It's okay. Just the fact that you said that much? That's a big deal. When you're ready… you'll know."

That night, I couldn't sleep. I lay awake thinking about how she didn't flinch. How she didn't judge. How, somehow, she just… got it. The next morning, she was gone. But on my bed, she'd left something behind: a cross necklace and a folded note.

Kaylynne,

I see the silence you carry. I used to carry it too. You don't have to hide forever. What happened to you was not your fault. But telling the truth—that's how you take your power back.

Speak up. Fight back. You're stronger than you think.

—Abby

P.S. This Cross necklace gave me courage. Now it's yours.

I sat on the edge of my bed, turning the necklace over in my hand, the words sinking in like water finding cracks in stone. Maybe she was right. Maybe it *was* time to try.

PART 2

**Strength is about finding the courage to speak
up about things you never thought you could.**

CHAPTER 13

Text Messages

The drive home was silent. My parents barely spoke, and the soft hum of the radio filled the car. I didn't mind the quiet, but the silence held weight. When we got home, I couldn't shake the feeling that I had let them down. They didn't ask questions about my time in the hospital, and I didn't offer answers. It felt like we all just wanted to forget.

Even though I understood why safety plans were in place—hiding medications, removing sharp objects, calling 911 if things got bad—I hated it. I hated the reminder that this wasn't a typical teenage life. I hated that it had to be mine.

The next evening, my dad took me for a drive. He was clearly trying to keep things light, filling the car with small talk to keep my mind from slipping back into darker places. I nodded along, staring out the window, but my thoughts were heavy. Everything felt different—strained. And it all felt like it was because of me. As we sat at a red light, he glanced at my red crop top and casually said, "You know, sometimes guys out there see things like that and get the wrong idea. Not saying it's right—but it happens."

A flicker of discomfort ran through me. "So?" I replied, masking my voice.

He went on. "There are guys out there who take advantage of girls. Not all men, but still."

"I know." My voice was even, but inside I was screaming. *It's already happened!* I didn't say it, though. I couldn't. His words felt like blame—like I was the reason it happened. I kept my fake smile steady, even though I was burning inside. I wanted to scream at him: How dare you make me feel like it's my fault?

Two days later, I returned to the psych ward after a short home visit. The psychiatrist deemed me fit for discharge, and I was relieved to leave. But the trauma of the ward followed me. I couldn't forget the handcuffs, the seclusion room, the male guards removing my clothes. It haunted me.

Back in my room, I sat holding the cross necklace Abby had given me, surrounded by familiar things that no longer brought comfort. My Taekwondo medals, old belts, certificates—once a symbol of who I was—now felt like hollow reminders. I wanted to be that girl again, the one who never gave up. But she felt lost.

I feared being taken from my home because of my mental health. I didn't want to lose myself completely. But loving myself? I couldn't imagine it anymore. Still, something in me wanted to try. It had been over a year since the rape in November 2018. I had kept it buried, swallowed by shame and rage. I wanted to believe I was healing, but I was breaking.

Then came December 27th, 2019. A message popped up on social media from a fake profile: "Those cuts on your whole body are absolutely disgusting." I threw my phone across the room.

Rage surged through me as I stormed to my room and screamed, "I fucking hate my life!"

My mom rushed in just as I grabbed a blade. "What's happening?" she asked, panicked.

"Leave me alone! I want to kill myself!" I shouted. She called my dad, and together they stopped me from hurting myself again. They had no choice but to call 911.

Back at the psych ward, I was numb. I spent New Year's there—again—avoiding everyone. Another failure. Another cycle. As months passed, I couldn't escape my triggers. Sirens, flashing lights, police cars—everything dragged me into flashbacks. People assumed I was okay, but I wanted to disappear. And then I remembered Abby. The girl who gave me the necklace. Maybe meeting her meant something—like a reminder that I wasn't alone. But how could I tell anyone the truth when I couldn't even say it to myself? That night, lying in bed, I had a thought: no one would believe me if I told them in person. But maybe if I had proof…

So I made a fake account. I typed the things he said to me, sending them to myself. It wasn't right. But it felt like the only way someone might believe me. I fell asleep at 2:00 a.m., hoping it would all make sense in the morning. But when I woke up, panic set in. I couldn't show anyone the messages.

A few days later, my mom got a call—I had finally been accepted into the DBT program. Everyone had said it could help. I wasn't sure. Therapy never really worked for me. Still, I agreed to meet with the psychiatrist.

In his office, I talked more than I expected to. He seemed different—present, kind. He believed DBT could help me, and he explained the support system it came with. I didn't trust it, but I agreed.

January 9, 2020. My first session. I was assigned to the same psychiatrist I had spoken with. For the first time in a long time, I felt safe around a man. Slowly, I opened up. Part of the DBT program included being able to contact him in moments of crisis, and I did. Knowing I had that option gave me a small sense of security I hadn't felt before.

One day, I walked into his office, unable to speak. I handed him my phone. He scrolled through the fake messages, and I sat there in silence, drowning in guilt. Then I said it:

"I was raped. I kept it a secret for over a year." I showed him my cuts. "This is why I self-harm. Nothing helps. Not therapy. Not meds. I just want it to stop."

He looked me in the eyes. "Kaylynne, this is not your fault. I believe you." Part of me thought he only believed me because of the messages. But hearing those words—*I believe you*—lifted some-thing from me. For the first time in a long time, I could breathe. But that breath was short. Because I was under 18, he had to tell my parents.

They were shocked. I couldn't look at them. My dad's face twisted in anger—not at me, but still hard to face. He asked me to go to the police. I begged him not to. I couldn't do it. He pointed out the 'evidence,' not knowing it was fake. I stayed silent. My mom didn't say much. Her silence said everything—confused, overwhelmed, unsure how to process it.

But at least they finally knew. And for the first time, I didn't have to carry it alone.

CHAPTER 14

It's Real When The Truth Comes Out

After over a year of hiding the truth, I finally told my parents. I thought I'd feel lighter—that the weight I carried would lift. But instead, it shattered me. The truth didn't heal me; it cracked something open. Their faces said everything: shock, sadness, confusion. I knew they wanted to help, but they didn't know how. I hoped they'd see that all my pain wasn't just depression—it was the result of what had been done to me. But I still couldn't tell them everything. He was still hurting me, and I wasn't ready to say it out loud.

Taekwondo had always been my escape. It was my source of happiness, a place where trust was built through sweat, focus, and connection. But after what happened, even walking into the academy made my heart race. I felt like an outsider, even among people I'd known for years. Trust didn't come easily anymore—until I opened up to my Master Instructor about my self-harm. Her response wasn't judgment. It wasn't disbelief. It was compassion. That moment changed everything. She became more than just a Master instructor—she came a lifeline. She listened, without trying to fix me. That kind of trust meant more than words could ever say.

Still, something inside me shifted after telling my parents. I had waited so long to be heard, but now that they knew, I almost wished they didn't. The safety of silence had been replaced by the chaos of reality. I spent most days curled up in my room, hiding from the world. I barely moved, barely ate. Time became meaningless. My body ached from exhaustion, and I couldn't find the strength to care about anything.

Therapy didn't help. My psychiatrist knew what happened, but I didn't think he truly understood. I felt like a lost cause. Every day felt heavier than the last. I wanted to disappear. My parents tried their best—they suggested movies, tried to engage me in small ways—but I couldn't pretend. Even watching TV became unbearable. A scene, just seconds long, triggered memories I fought to keep buried. I left the room before the tears could fall.

Flashbacks took over. The sounds, smells, and faces around me all became triggers. I couldn't walk outside without seeing someone who reminded me of him. So I stayed inside. My room became a prison I didn't want to leave.

The weight of my parents' questions didn't help. They wanted answers. Details. But I couldn't go back there—not again. Every question was a wound reopened. I knew they meant well, but their search for answers only made me feel more broken.

February brought my sixteenth birthday—a day that should've felt like a celebration. But I didn't feel sixteen. I didn't feel anything. I was numb. And guilty. I believed I had ruined everything for my parents. All the hospital visits, the fear, the pain—I thought it was all my fault. By mid-February, the urge to end my life was back.

I reached out to my psychiatrist. He tried to help, but I couldn't follow his plan. Nothing made sense. So I was admitted to the psych ward. Again.

February 19th arrived—the day of my black belt test—and I was still in the psych ward. I sat in a sterile hospital room, watching the minutes crawl by, convinced I was going to miss the one thing I had worked so hard for. All the years of dedication, all the pain I had pushed through—it felt like it was about to be taken from me. But then I told the psychiatrist what that test meant to me, how much I had poured into it. Something changed in that moment. He saw it in my eyes. He understood.

He let me go. I walked out of the psych ward with a nervous, grateful heart. I was free—for now. I didn't tell anyone where I had been. I just focused on what mattered: earning that belt. That night, I sat on the edge of the mat, waiting for my name to be called. "Kaylynne Venn," my Master Instructor announced. I stood, bowed, answering yes sir and stepped forward.

The test pushed me to my limit. Every muscle screamed, every breath felt like fire—but I refused to stop. Each movement came from a place deeper than training—it came from everything I had survived. I wasn't just showing my technique—I was showing that I was still here. Still fighting. Still standing.

And when it ended, I knew: I had done it. That black belt became more than a symbol. It was proof that I could overcome, even when everything in me wanted to give up. It reminded me that strength isn't always loud. Sometimes, it's just refusing to stay down.

On that mat, I didn't just earn a belt—I reclaimed a part of myself I thought was gone. And for the first time in a long time, I felt proud of who I was becoming.

CHAPTER 15

Hold On To Hope

As I stepped through the door of my house, exhaustion crept into the very core of my being. The floor let out its familiar creak as I made my way toward my bedroom. I lay on my bed, expecting the usual nightmares to creep in. But instead, I was met with something unfamiliar: peace. A strange, still calm settled over me—a calm I hadn't felt since the rape.

For a moment, I didn't know how to feel. I had become so used to sadness and anxiety that their absence felt wrong. The silence inside me was unsettling. I had spent so long drowning that floating suddenly felt unnatural.

I lay there, unsure if I should lean into the relief or cling to the pain I'd come to know. The next morning, something felt different. I stared at the ceiling, trying to understand what had changed. Was this healing? Did I deserve it? Or was it just another illusion? I didn't feel sadness, but I didn't feel joy either. Just stillness. It was like everything had dried up inside me. No tears. No smiles. Just dust.

As time passed, a wave of memories rose again—ghosts I thought I had pushed away. The images weren't sharp, but they lingered at the edge of my thoughts. I could feel a shift—a rope that had tied me to my past had finally snapped. I didn't understand why it happened now, but something inside me had let go.

I stood and walked to the mirror on my wall. I stared at the reflection looking back at me. The shame, regret, and misery that had weighed me down felt lighter. But a new fear replaced them: *Who am I without my pain?* I asked myself if I'd always be defined by trauma. I'd spent so long wearing the label of 'suicidal' and 'mentally ill' that I wasn't sure who I was underneath it.

After what Noah did to me, I spent every moment trying to protect my family from my pain. I stayed quiet, even when it nearly killed me. But once the truth came out, I realized how deeply it impacted them, too. The trauma wasn't just mine anymore—it had become a shared weight.

Watching them carry it made something shift in me. I couldn't stay silent forever. I needed to heal. But before I could begin, I had to learn how to fight the demons inside me—the ones that still whispered that I wasn't worth saving. And how could I fight them if I wasn't even willing to talk about it in therapy?

Then something unexpected happened. A flicker of hope—small, but real—settled inside me. I had spent so long chasing happiness that I forgot what it felt like. The girl I used to be seemed like a ghost. And yet, in some strange way, this new version of me felt more real than anything I'd ever known.

In the darkest hours, I had grown used to the company of depression, anxiety, and nightmares. They became part of me. I let hope slip through my fingers once, thinking I was beyond saving. But as much as I wanted to sink again, something stopped me. I walked into the living room and stared out the window. My mom walked in and looked at me. "Are you okay?" she asked.

"Yeah, why are you asking?" I replied.

"Just making sure," she said, sitting down and turning on the TV.

The truth was, I didn't know if I was okay. My thoughts were still dark. The risk of self-harm still lingered. But something—something

I couldn't explain—was keeping me from letting go. Maybe it was hope. Maybe it was a survival instinct. Or maybe it was God. Even though I don't consider myself very religious, part of me believes He was showing me that a new path was still possible.

I wasn't healed. But for the first time, I saw that healing might be possible.

CHAPTER 16

Attention Seeker

As the calendar turned to February 24th, 2020, Monday arrived with a heaviness I couldn't shake. The thought of returning to school gripped me with fear. Now that my parents finally knew the truth, they understood why I had been refusing to go. I could see the guilt on their faces—how hard it was for them to realize they had unknowingly sent me back into an unsafe place.

They didn't want me to return, but it wasn't really a choice. The school I was attending was the closest to our house, and at the time, my parents didn't know how to go about switching schools. It wasn't that they didn't care—they were doing everything they could to make sure I would be safe. The guidance counsellor reassured them that Noah would be kept away from me and even said that he wasn't really coming to school anymore. So my parents trusted the school's plan, hoping it would be enough to protect me.

When my mom spoke with the school's guidance counsellor to explain everything and ask how they would keep me safe, what she heard left her stunned: "I think he likes her, and she just doesn't know how to react," the counsellor said. Still, they promised to take steps to protect me, reassuring her again that he wasn't really coming to school anymore.

I returned to school. Noah wasn't there, at least not on that first day, which brought some relief. But it didn't erase the fear that lingered beneath my skin. I kept looking over my shoulder, never sure if he'd show up anyway. At my locker, my hands shook as I fumbled with the combination. I heard two students whisper behind me. "She obviously has a knack for drawing attention to herself," one of them said. I pulled down my sleeves, hiding the scars, and walked away to the back doors. I sank into a corner, curling into myself.

This kind of thing became normal. Students stared, pointed, whispered. Eventually, I stopped covering my scars. That's when the messages started—DMs from classmates accusing me of seeking attention and saying I should be locked away in a mental hospital. Their words weren't just cruel—they followed me home, deepening the shame I was already fighting.

The bell rang, but I stayed on the floor until a resource teacher found me. "You need to get to class," she said. I didn't move. "If you don't want to go to class, come to the resource room," she added, gently. I followed her. The room was quiet. Then, she walked in—a girl I'd never really spoken to but definitely recognized. She was the one who always called me names in the halls—attention seeker, crazy, broken. We had never had a real conversation, yet she always had something to say.

She sat across from me, looked confused, and handed me an envelope. "It's from Noah," she said, like even she didn't understand why he had asked her to give it to me.

My voice trembled. "Please, just give me space." She paused for a moment, clearly uncomfortable, then slid the envelope toward me. I tore it open without even looking at what was inside.

She stared for a second, then muttered coldly, "You're so desperate for attention," before turning and walking away. Her words stung—sharp and cruel, like she had no idea the damage they could do.

My heart raced. What was in that letter? I would never know. Consumed by a mix of anger and pain, I grabbed my bag and ran. I locked myself in a bathroom stall, pulled out a sharp object, and gave in to the only relief I knew. I sat on the cold floor, cutting, numbing. Time passed until a knock came. "Kaylynne, I need you to come out," the resource teacher said.

Leave me alone," I mumbled.

"I'm not leaving." Eventually, I unlocked the door. One look at me, and she knew. "I'm taking you to the office," she said. She walked me straight to the guidance counsellor's office. The moment I sat down, the counsellor shifted into a tone of concern, asking if I was okay and trying to talk to me like she cared. But all I could think about was how she had dismissed me the first time I told her I had been touched inappropriately—how she looked past it like it was nothing. And now she cared?

I left, the rage boiling over. I ran home, my legs burning, my lungs aching. I burst through the side door, past my mom's worried questions, straight into my room. Just days ago, I had felt hope. Now, it was gone.

Why did I have more bad days than good ones? Why did pain always return? I grabbed a bag and told my mom I needed to go for a walk. She tried to stop me, but I ran. At the park, I sat on the steps of an elementary school with a plan in my bag. I watched the children run and laugh. Their joy was so simple. I missed that. I remembered something my psychiatrist had said: "You don't have to die to solve your problems. If you work hard, you can find a life worth living."

I called him. I told him what I was thinking. He tried to help me use DBT skills. I wanted to listen—but I was too far gone. The call stretched on. Eventually, he said, "I think we need to get the police involved."

"No," I begged. "Please don't. I can keep myself safe."

But he didn't believe me. As the call continued, I took what I had hidden in my hand. He didn't know. He stayed on the phone, even as I begged him to go. "You probably have more important things to do."

He stayed until the police arrived. Two officers walked up to me. "Are you Kaylynne?" one asked.

I nodded and handed him my phone. "It's my psychiatrist. He wants to talk to you."

After the call ended, the officer looked at me. "You need to go to the hospital." I wanted to run. But I couldn't. I got into the back of the police car, arms crossed, silent. The officer tried to talk. I ignored him—until he asked, "What could bring a smile to your face?"

I whispered, "Coffee."

He smiled. "Let's go grab you a coffee." Before I stepped into the hospital, he looked at me and said, "Life can be cruel, but don't lose hope. Your future holds endless possibilities. Don't give up on yourself, Kaylynne."

Inside, my mom was already there. A doctor came quickly, asking, "Did you take anything?" I said no. Eventually, a psychiatrist came. I told him what I thought he wanted to hear. That I was safe. That I had therapy tomorrow. It was enough to let me go home. The ride back was silent. At home, I climbed into bed, the weight of everything crashing down on me.

I had survived another crisis—but just barely.

CHAPTER 17

PTSD

As my mom drove me to my psychiatrist appointment, the sunlight filtered through the window, casting a warm, golden glow. But it didn't reach me. I had woken up with the weight of the previous night still clinging to me, my body aching with the aftermath of everything I had endured. Each step toward the hospital felt heavy, like my bones carried every moment of pain from the night before.

In the waiting room, I sat in silence until my psychiatrist appeared and waved for me to follow him. We walked down the hall to his office and sat across from each other. He didn't say anything at first, but something in his expression told me he already knew. There was a shift in the air—something unspoken passing between us, heavier than words. He finally broke it, gently asking me what had happened the day before. I looked down, my voice barely a whisper. "I can't explain it... it just happened."

He nodded with understanding. "I may not know everything, but I understand you're trying to end the pain. I want you to know something—something I need you to hear. I care about you, Kaylynne. I would be heartbroken if you were gone. You don't need to die to fix your problems. I'm here to help you through them."

I looked up, confused.

He leaned back in his chair and added, "Ten years from now, I don't think you'll still be facing the same struggles."

I didn't believe him. I couldn't. Anger boiled inside me. "You'll never truly understand what I've been through." I started telling him everything. All the ways the trauma had shattered my life.

And then he said it—four letters that shook me to my core: "It sounds like you have PTSD."

A chill ran through me. Deep down, I knew it. But hearing it out loud made it real. Made it permanent. I didn't want it. I didn't want another label. But then he explained the symptoms. Flashbacks. Panic attacks. Emotional spirals. Avoiding places. And then a word I had never heard before—dissociation.

He explained it slowly, using examples. The more he spoke, the more I realized I'd been living with it. That detached, numb feeling I couldn't put into words—this was it. Finally, things started to make sense. Then a thought slipped out of my mouth before I could stop it. "I can't help but wonder… if I were very underweight, maybe nobody would want to rape me."

He opened his mouth, but I cut him off. "It was just a thought." What he didn't know was that I had recently started eating less and hiding it. I smiled at the dinner table like everything was fine, but sometimes I'd excuse myself to go to the bathroom just to undo what I'd eaten. It wasn't something I had done before, but lately, I had started looking at my reflection differently—studying my body with a mix of shame and control I didn't fully understand.

I looked down at the floor as he kept speaking. My fingers tapped nervously against the armrest. And then, in the quietest voice, I said something I never thought I'd say to a male mental health professional. "I want to work on what happened to me."

He paused, then looked directly at me. "Do you think you're ready to talk about it?"

The anxiety churned in my stomach. I knew opening that door would hurt. It would tear things open again. But somehow, I said it anyway. "Yes."

He explained exposure therapy. I'd have to record myself talking about the trauma for 30 minutes, then listen to it repeatedly at home. I'd also need to confront the things that triggered me—like being hugged, being in big crowds, or looking at the pool where it happened.

Just as I started to wrap my head around it, he added something that made my heart sink: "Before we can begin, you need to be self-harm free for two months."

Two months. That felt impossible. I gripped my phone tighter, feeling the blades hidden in the back of the case pressing against my fingertips.

And I wondered, for the first time, if I could really let them go.

CHAPTER 18

Battling The Demons In My Head

A rush of determination ran through me as I stood in front of my mirror. A few days had passed since my conversation with the psychiatrist. The weight of my past pressed heavily on my shoulders. The awareness hit me like a lightning bolt, igniting a fire within. This time, it was different. I truly wanted to change—a burning desire to grow into a better version of myself. Yet, reality settled in. If I wanted to do exposure therapy, I would have to stop self-harming. Oddly, those very acts seemed to keep me from slipping away entirely.

That day, I made a promise. I stood in front of the mirror, my body marked with scars, and made a promise to stop self-harming. I wanted to do this for my parents—to stop the constant worry, to hear my mom laugh again, to feel like my dad was emotionally present again. But mostly, I needed this for me. Because I couldn't keep surviving by hurting myself to feel alive. Because deep down, I knew if I didn't fight for myself now, I might not get another chance. I wasn't just trying to break a habit—I was trying to break free from a cycle that had nearly swallowed me whole.

I had already visited the emergency room fifteen times for a mental health crisis and been admitted to the psych ward seven times since the rape. Something had to change. I stood in front of the trash can, hands trembling, and let go of the objects that had once brought relief. The blades dropped one by one. My anxiety spiked, but I turned away. I grabbed my phone and called my psychiatrist, desperate to not go back.

Calling him became a lifeline. Day or night, his voice cut through the fog in my mind. I always apologized for calling, but he never made me feel like a burden. "You don't need to be sorry," he said. His reassurance helped me believe I was worth saving. Even when I couldn't believe in myself, he believed in me enough to get me through one more moment. Sometimes, that was all I needed.

Then came March 2020. COVID-19 locked down the world and trapped me inside with my own thoughts. School moved online. I couldn't focus. Depression weighed heavier. I stopped attending Zoom classes and slept the days away.

Each morning, I stared at the pills I took. They were supposed to help, but I only felt more drained. When I learned some antidepressants caused weight gain, panic took over. I didn't want to eat. I didn't want to feel full. I just wanted control. My relationship with my body and food became a battlefield—a silent war that I didn't know how to stop fighting.

Therapy moved to Zoom too. But the screen felt empty. I missed the comfort of my psychiatrist's office. Even group sessions online made me feel alone. I would stare at the screen, watching everyone's pixelated faces, trying to force connection where it no longer existed.

I kept telling myself that I had made a promise. That I had thrown the blades away. But I never knew how hard it would be to live up to a decision when my brain was screaming for relief. I wanted to stop. I truly did. But stopping wasn't clean. It wasn't easy. It didn't happen overnight. Every moment I didn't hurt myself was a battle against a body that had been trained to believe pain meant safety.

The urge to self-harm crept back in. I tried everything: snapping elastics, drawing red lines on my skin with a pen, gripping ice cubes.

Some things helped. Most didn't. But I kept trying. I journaled, I drew, I screamed into pillows. I paced back and forth across my bedroom floor, whispering reminders that I was stronger than this. Some nights I won. Some nights, I didn't.

There were times I caught myself obsessing over my food, tricking myself into thinking I was 'just being healthy' when really, I was feeding my need for control. Some days I skipped meals without even meaning to. Other days, I couldn't let myself eat until I had earned it. It was like I was playing a game I hadn't agreed to—one with rules that kept changing, and no way to win.

By June 3rd, 2020, I had gone a month without self-harming. After three long months of trying, that milestone mattered. I finally felt proud. But then the phone calls started. Unknown numbers flooded my phone. I ignored them at first. Then I picked up. It was him. "I'm sorry about everything," he said. "I love you. I just want you to be happy."

My body froze. I wanted to scream, but all I could say was, "I will never be with you after what you did."

His voice turned cold. "I'll be outside your window. Watching. With a gun." Panic clamped around my chest. Maybe he was lying. But maybe he wasn't.

I didn't feel safe in my own home. I started checking my windows. I jumped at shadows. I slept with the lights on.

The thoughts came back. I held a sharp object, my hands shaking. I thought of the month I had fought for, the people I didn't want to disappoint. I forced myself upstairs. "I'm reaching my breaking point," I told my mom. "Just take me to the hospital."

It was the first time I asked to go. I needed to protect that one-month milestone. I didn't want to lose the progress I had fought for. At the hospital, my anxiety skyrocketed. COVID patients filled the waiting area. But I knew I was doing the right thing.

Eventually, I saw the same psychiatrist I had worked with in the past. I felt safer opening up to him. I told him everything. He gently asked if I wanted to report the assault. "No," I said. "I'm not ready." He respected that. He also noted how withdrawn I seemed—a change he recorded in my file. The world felt unsafe. I thought that if I disappeared, maybe I wouldn't get hurt again.

I was admitted again. It was a short stay. The next morning, I sat down with the psychiatrist again. I didn't hold back this time. I talked about the fear, the triggers, the threats, and how I felt like I was unravelling. I told him how everything felt like too much, how I wasn't sure how to keep going without falling back into old patterns. He listened without interruption, his face calm but alert, taking in every word.

And for the first time, I didn't feel like a case file or a diagnosis. I felt like a person—one who still had a voice.

Then the psychiatrist asked, "Has this ever been reported to Child and Family Services?"

I shook my head. "No."

"Because of what you've shared, I'm required by law to make a report to Child and Family Services," he said gently. "I know this might be hard to hear, but our responsibility is to ensure your safety."

I froze. "No! I don't want them involved! That should be my choice."

The nurses tried to explain. "We're mandated to report any disclosure of sexual violence." I felt the air leave my lungs.

One nurse said, "Even if charges aren't filed, someone might speak with him. It might help end contact."

"Why didn't my psychiatrist report it before?" I asked.

"We got in touch with him," she said gently. "He thought it had already been taken care of and didn't realize it hadn't. It wasn't anything intentional—he genuinely believed the report had already been made."

I felt betrayed. I didn't want anyone talking to Noah. I didn't want to make things worse. The fear was suffocating. I tried to convince them I could go home. The psychiatrist said, "We'll see how you feel tomorrow."

But I couldn't wait. I called my mom, begging her to get me out. She came to the hospital and talked to the psychiatrist. They agreed I could leave, but I had to create a safety plan. And just like that, I knew I couldn't avoid what came next: a call from Child and Family Services.

CHAPTER 19

Finding My Voice

J ust when I thought things couldn't get more overwhelming, I had already been told that Child and Family Services had been contacted without my consent. I felt blindsided.

The idea of having to share my story again—especially with people I didn't know—tightened the knot in my stomach. It felt like control over my own story was being taken from me all over again.

The shame that followed was suffocating. I blamed myself for what had happened, and now, someone else would hear the truth I had barely spoken aloud.

It felt like standing at the base of a mountain made of every fear I'd ever known—shame, guilt, rage, and the desperate need to be believed. Climbing it seemed impossible.

One morning, my mom got a call. I watched her answer it, her eyes softening as she listened. A CFS worker wanted to speak with me—either at their office or in our home. "What do you want to do?" she asked gently.

My chest tightened. "At home," I said. I needed the comfort of my own space, even if I wasn't sure I'd be able to speak. A few days later, she arrived. Her name was Anna. She smiled warmly as she stepped into our living room. My parents left us alone, and I sat there, barely breathing.

She told me I didn't have to talk unless I wanted to. My voice cracked: "What's the point? It happened over a year ago."

Her reply: "It doesn't matter when it happened. What matters is that it did—and that you're strong enough to talk about it now."

Her calmness made me feel something I hadn't felt in a long time—safe. Words I hadn't planned to say started spilling out. I told her about the first rape. I braced for judgment, but all she said was, "I believe you." That phrase—so simple—hit harder than anything else. I had waited over a year to hear those words from someone in power. But even as she said them, doubt echoed in my mind. It felt like maybe she only said it because it was her job to. I hesitated, then reached for my phone and showed her the fake texts I had created—proof I thought I needed to be believed. She looked at them, then looked at me. "I believed you even before this," she said.

Then she said, "I will need to speak with Noah—to warn him to stay away from you." My stomach dropped. I asked her not to, the fear rising in my throat. She assured me I'd be protected and reminded me I could call 911 if I ever felt unsafe. But the reassurance didn't settle the unease growing inside me.

Later, during an online therapy session, the guilt caught up with me. I confessed everything to my psychiatrist—that the texts were fake, that I had created them out of desperation. I expected him to be angry. He wasn't. "That thought didn't even cross my mind," he said. "You've shown more honesty in admitting this than most people ever could."

After the session ended, I called Anna. It was one of the hardest phone calls I've ever made. She wasn't just anyone—she represented a system, a person in power. And for someone like me, who had been repeatedly silenced and doubted, reaching out to her felt terrifying. But I knew she needed to hear the truth.

When she answered, her voice was steady and kind. I braced myself and told her everything. She listened without judgment. "You're not the first to do this," she said gently, her voice steady and full of understanding.

"When someone hasn't been believed, especially after something traumatic, it's not uncommon for them to try to create proof—anything that might make someone finally listen. It doesn't make your truth any less real. It makes you human."

Her words wrapped around me like a soft blanket—finally, someone understood. "What matters," she said, "is that you came forward. That takes courage."

I told her I was scared my parents would be angry. So she came back to our house and spoke with them. She explained why survivors sometimes try to create proof—because we're terrified that the truth won't be enough. When she finished, silence fell. I braced for anger. Instead, my parents looked at me and said, "We believe you."

That moment changed me. For the first time, I wasn't hiding behind a lie. I wasn't using pain to speak for me. I had said the truth—and been believed. But even in that pride, something shifted. After speaking the truth and hearing so many people say they believed me, something inside me stirred—something that felt like courage.

For the first time, I considered going to the police not because I was told to, but because I wanted to. The thought of doing it still terrified me, and it stirred up another spiral that led to yet another hospital visit on July 9th, 2020. But even through the fear, the idea stayed with me. I wasn't just surviving anymore—I was starting to reclaim my voice.

Lying in the psych ward, I realized how much I had survived. I didn't want to be a victim anymore. I was ready to stop blaming myself. I wanted to speak up—not just for me, but for others like me. The next day, I walked into a police station. My parents were by my side. I couldn't speak. My mom did. We sat in the waiting area. My whole body trembled. I almost backed out. But I didn't.

A female detective stepped into the waiting room and called my name. Her tone was calm but professional, and everything about her presence reminded me that this was real. My parents and I stood together as we followed her through a series of quiet hallways. Eventually, we stopped in front of a door labeled 'Family Room.'

The detective turned to my parents and gently explained that they would wait there while she took me to another room to begin the interview. My parents gave me a small, worried smile before stepping inside. I turned to follow the detective down one more hallway, my legs shaky beneath me. Each step felt heavier than the last as we approached the door where my story would finally be told.

Someone from the department was in a separate room, monitoring the interview and operating the recording equipment. The room I was in felt different from what I expected. It wasn't cold or clinical—it was warm and comforting, designed to help someone like me feel safe enough to speak.

There was a soft couch with pillows, a single chair across from it, and a small table with a box of Kleenex resting on top. I chose the couch and sank into it, trying to calm the shaking in my hands. The detective took the chair across from me, her eyes meeting mine with gentle seriousness.

Her voice was steady as she said, "Before we begin, I need you to promise that everything you tell me will be the truth."

I swallowed hard, the lump in my throat nearly choking me. But I managed to nod. "Yes," I whispered. I told her everything. When I finished, she asked if I had anything more to add. Tears streamed down my face. I told her about the fake texts.

She didn't flinch. She just said it again: "I believe you."

It had taken more than an hour. I was exhausted, but proud. I had done it. I had reported the rape. Before I left, she said, "I'm proud of you." She touched my shoulder and added, "It's going to be okay."

Back in the hallway with my parents, she explained what would happen next. The investigation could take a year or more—a timeline that crushed me. I had just found the strength to speak, and now I had to wait. I wanted it all to be over. I wanted closure, answers, justice. But instead, I was told to be patient. It was hard news to hear. Still, something in me had changed. For the first time, I wasn't silent. I was fighting back.

PART 3

It's in the darkest moments that resilience is born. The journey to healing is not always easy, but it's in facing the brokenness that we discover it's always worth it.

CHAPTER 20

To Myself, Who Can Win This Fight

After filing the police report, I expected relief. Instead, a storm of emotions rushed in—first pride, then doubt, and then a darkness I thought I had already escaped. The thought of him walking away without consequences lit a fire in me. I had come too far to let him silence me again. Justice became my anchor—the one thing I could still fight for.

One day, I remembered something a nurse had once told me during my time in the psych ward: *Write a letter to yourself. Something kind. Something honest.* At the time, I dismissed it. But now, I found myself pulling out my journal. Maybe I needed to hear something I hadn't told myself in a long time.

I sat at my desk, gripping a pen tightly in my hand. I didn't know exactly what I was about to write, but somehow, my hand started to move.

To myself, who can win this fight,

You've been through hell, and it's nothing short of a miracle that you're still here. I know the darkness feels heavy, unbearable even. But please— stay. You have more to see. More to do. Your light hasn't gone out. It's still there, even if it's flickering.

You were never the problem. The pain you carry was never yours to hold—it was put there by someone who had no right. But look at you. You're still here. And that means more than words can say. Your existence is proof that even in the deepest darkness, the human spirit can survive. You are living, breathing defiance against everything that tried to destroy you.

I believe in you. I love you. Please keep fighting.

—Yourself

I read it again and again. It didn't sound like me—at least not yet. But maybe it sounded like the person I was trying to become. The fact that I even wrote it down was something. And maybe that was enough for now.

In the following days, I kept returning to that letter. It reminded me that even when everything felt out of control, I was still choosing to try. And that mattered.

Healing didn't come in a straight line. Every time I talked to someone about what happened—especially with people close to me—it felt like tearing open a wound that had just begun to scab. Sometimes I wanted to run from it all.

Other times, I wanted to scream. But I stayed. I stayed because I knew silence wouldn't set me free. And every time I showed up, I proved to myself that I could survive it.

During a virtual session with my psychiatrist, I finally said the words out loud: "I want to live—but I don't know how."

He nodded gently. "That makes sense," he said. "There are ways we can work on helping you want to live again. It won't happen all at once, but we can take steps—starting with the things that make it hardest."

I didn't hesitate. "It's the nightmares," I said quietly. "They don't stop. I go to bed afraid and wake up more exhausted than when I closed my eyes. I want to live, but not like this."

He took a moment, then said, "There's a medication that specifically targets trauma-related nightmares. It might not take them away completely, but it can help reduce how often they happen—and how intense they are. Would you be willing to try it?"

I hesitated. Medications had always been a frustrating cycle of trial and error—some that made me feel numb or disconnected too much, others that left me feeling nothing.

But this time, something inside me said, *Try again.* "Okay," I said. "I'll try."

Eventually, we found a medication that didn't numb me. It didn't fix everything, but it helped me find balance. Enough to start looking forward instead of drowning in the past. Therapy began to shift in ways I hadn't expected. One day, my psychiatrist looked at me and said, "I can see how hard you're working—not just in here, but out there in your life, too."

Those words stayed with me. *Making an effort.* Maybe that was everything. For the first time in a long time, I believed him. I had gone two whole months without self-harming. Two months of showing up to DBT sessions. Two months of choosing myself, even when it was hard.

That's when we began exposure therapy. It terrified me. The idea of talking about the trauma in detail felt like too much. Sometimes I dissociated mid-session. Other times, I froze—but I kept going and slowly, something shifted. Talking didn't erase the pain—but it helped me strip away the shame. It helped me see that what happened to me was something I lived through—not something that defined me, owned me, or could ever take away who I am at my core.

Eventually, we talked about the behaviours I'd developed—the fears, the flashbacks, the things I avoided without even realizing it. DBT gave me tools. Exposure therapy gave me courage. Change didn't happen all at once. But in small moments, I saw it: When I took a deep breath through a trigger instead of panicking. When I looked in the mirror and, for the first time in years, didn't hate the girl staring back.

And maybe the biggest sign of all: I had hope. Not every day. Not all the time. But I had it. I was learning to live again. The war wasn't over. But I was no longer losing.

CHAPTER 21

You Can't Give Up

One day, while browsing articles online, I came across a story that stopped me in my tracks. It was about a survivor of sexual violence who had found her way forward—not by forgetting her past, but by refusing to let it define her. Her journey lit something in me. For the first time in a long time, I felt the quiet rise of hope. Not the kind that shouts, but the kind that stirs deep inside and says, *Maybe there's more waiting for me on the other side of this*. I began to wonder if one day I could be the reason someone else believes in their own strength. But first, I had to fight for mine.

On the morning of July 24th, 2020, I felt off the moment I opened my eyes. There wasn't one specific symptom—just a heaviness in my body and a sense that something was wrong. I wandered into the living room, trying to shake it off.

My dad was already up. "How was your sleep?" he asked casually.

"It was okay," I replied, settling across from him. "But I don't feel right."

He raised an eyebrow. "What's wrong?"

I hesitated. "I don't know," I said honestly, because I didn't. But whatever it was, it was building fast. Suddenly, the room spun. My heart pounded. Everything blurred.

A wave of panic hit, followed by a flash of memory—I had felt this before. "I just had an absent seizure," I said, panic tightening my chest.

My dad stared at me, stunned. "You haven't had one since you were seven. Are you sure?"

"I'm sure." He called for my mom. As she tried to reach the neurologist, I grew more dis-oriented. "I want to go to the hospital," I said. I never asked to go unless I knew something was really wrong.

At the hospital, we barely waited before I was brought to a bed. I remember lying there, my body growing heavier by the minute. Everything started to feel distant, like I was slipping out of the moment. Then—nothing. A blank space where time dis-appeared.

The next thing I remember was opening my eyes to a nurse standing beside me. "Hi, my name is Jamie. Do you know where you are?"

I didn't. I was exhausted and confused, struggling to piece together where I was and how I got there. "You just had a seizure," she explained gently. I blinked at her, trying to make sense of the words. Up until now, my seizures had never taken away my awareness. I had always been present, always remembered. But this—this was different. And that difference filled me with fear I hadn't felt before.

Then another seizure hit. And another. My limbs flailed uncontrollably, jerking with a force I couldn't control. I cried out without meaning to, overwhelmed by pain and panic. My body ached from the tension, and I could barely catch my breath between the waves. Nurses and doctors surrounded me, trying multiple rounds of rescue medications. None of them worked. I saw the concern deepen in their eyes as time passed.

Four and a half hours later—after what felt like a marathon of fear, confusion, and unanswered questions—they made the decision to admit me. It was clear this wasn't just a passing episode. Something much deeper was happening.

The next days blurred. I faded in and out, unsure if I was seizing or sleeping. I felt trapped—by my own body and by a fear I couldn't explain. Eventually, the nurses wheeled in equipment and began placing electrodes across my scalp, hooking me up to an EEG monitor. They explained it would track my brain's electrical activity for the next 24 hours to capture what was happening during my seizures.

But before the full observation even began, something shifted inside me. Everything changed. My body tensed, but this time it wasn't just convulsions. I had no control over what was happening—and even less awareness of what I was saying. From somewhere deep inside me, words burst out: raw, panicked cries like "stop" and "don't touch me." I wouldn't remember saying them, but my parents later told me. Hearing that shook me to my core.

Those weren't just random words—they were the echoes of a trauma I had buried so deep, even I didn't know how much of it still lived inside me. It was terrifying to learn that my body had screamed the things I had never been able to say out loud. All that fear, all that pain—it had been stored in silence. And now, it was forcing its way out, one seizure at a time.

This seizure wasn't just physical. It tore through every layer of me—emotionally, mentally, and physically. For two hours, my body and mind were overtaken by something I couldn't name, something far deeper than a medical condition. It was as if all the pain I had locked away, all the memories I had tried to silence, exploded all at once. My body became the voice for what I couldn't speak. It wasn't just a seizure—it was survival unravelling itself in real time. No one, not even me, had seen anything like it before.

When I came to, I was restrained, surrounded by security. A nurse explained I had been hitting the bed rails during the seizure, which had lasted nearly two hours. The restraints had been used to protect me throughout it. But all I felt was shame and confusion.

Then came the diagnosis: PNES—Psychogenic Nonepileptic Seizures. They weren't caused by abnormal brain activity like epilepsy, but they were just as real—only rooted in trauma instead of electricity. Part of me felt relief. I finally had a name for what was happening. But another part of me felt crushed. PNES came with misunderstanding, stigma, and silence.

If it had been epilepsy, people might've known how to respond. But this? This felt invisible. And being misunderstood hurt almost as much as the seizures themselves.

Despite everything, the hospital staff seemed eager to send me home. My parents' concerns were brushed off. "Non-medical," they said. We felt powerless. At the front entrance, just as we were about to leave, another seizure overwhelmed me. My legs gave out beneath me, and I collapsed. My body shook violently, drawing the attention of security.

My parents were frantic, trying to explain what was happening, their voices filled with panic and desperation. They didn't want to take me home—how could they? They had no idea how to support me through seizures like this. Nurses rushed in, and within moments, the head administrator appeared. She took one look at me—curled on the floor, barely conscious—and said firmly, "She's not going anywhere like this." In that moment, a decision was made. I was going to be readmitted.

The next thing I remember was waking up again—another unfamiliar moment in an all-too-familiar place. I was tired. Frustrated. And heartbroken. How could trauma do this to a body? The diagnosis of PNES forced me to face something I hadn't fully grasped before: trauma doesn't only live in the mind. It lives in the body, too. And my body had been carrying it for years.

I lay in the hospital bed, my mom sitting nearby. I didn't know what came next. But I kept whispering to myself, "You can't give up." After five days, I was sent home. The medical doctors barely interacted with me by the end—they saw the seizures as psychological, not medical. Because of that, they sent in a psychiatrist to speak with my parents. He briefly explained the PNES diagnosis and told them to 'keep an eye on her.'

That was it. No plan. No follow-up. Just fear, confusion, and the weight of not knowing what to do next. And yet, in the middle of all that confusion, something shifted inside me. I didn't want to let this be the end of my story. I wanted to prove—first to myself, and then to others—that even when life knocks you down, you can rise again. And fight.

That day planted a seed in me. Not of shame, but of purpose.

CHAPTER 22

Memories And Battles Of A Survivor

Still, a week after coming home from the hospital, the weight of everything began to crush me. I couldn't shake the feeling that I had failed—as a daughter, as a person, as someone trying to get better. For two years, I had been emotionally frozen since the trauma, and now, little by little, I was beginning to come back to life.

I had worked so hard to be the version of myself everyone needed—the good daughter, the strong survivor—but no matter how hard I tried, I couldn't outrun the memories. They kept coming back, one after another—the hospital, the self-harm, the time I almost ended everything. No matter how hard I tried, I couldn't escape them. I wanted to forget, but my brain wouldn't let me.

On impulse, I grabbed the last of my money and rushed out the door before my parents could stop me. I knew they were afraid—afraid I'd have another seizure—but I didn't care. I didn't tell them where I was going. I just knew I had to escape. I ran to the store with one goal in mind: make the thoughts stop.

Afterward, I wandered to a place I thought no one would find me. I held the object in my hand, the one I had just bought, and stared at it. "I promised myself I would never do this again," I whispered, tears slipping down my cheeks. Just then, something inside me stirred. A quiet voice—small, but there—said, *What if there's still hope?* And that was enough. I pulled out my phone and called my psychiatrist.

When he called back, I didn't wait. "Please help me! I don't know what I was thinking, but I spent all my money trying to end my life."

He listened calmly. "Kaylynne, I'm so sorry you're in that dark place. But like I've told you before—you don't have to die to solve your problems. I'm here. Do you still have what you bought?"

"Yeah. And I'm not tossing it out. I just spent all my money on it."

"I understand. But I truly want you to know—you matter. And if you weren't here, the world would feel that loss."

I looked down, silent. "I just spent all my money on it. I'm not going to throw it away. And besides... it's not like you actually care."

"No, Kaylynne. I mean it. You matter—and if what's stopping you is the money, then let's talk about that. How much did you pay for it?"

"Ten dollars. Why?"

"I'll give you ten dollars if you toss it out the next time we meet."

"You don't have to do that."

"I know. But I want to."

His kindness caught me off guard. We talked more after that, and the spiral I was in began to slow. I ended up throwing the object away—not because of the money, but because for the first time in a while, I did something for me. A small part of me wanted to live. Two days later, I sat across from him in his office. He asked, "Did you throw it away?"

"Yeah," I said, my eyes fixed on a spot behind him.

He pulled out a ten-dollar bill. "I knew you were strong enough." I stared at the money. "No, I can't take that."

"I'm not making you. But it's here if you want it." I took it slowly. It wasn't just money. It was a reminder that someone believed in me. That I mattered. That I wasn't alone. In that space, something shifted. I began to open up more—first to him, then to myself.

For so long, this had been a silent part of my struggle, something I didn't even know how to explain. But after everything that had just happened—the near relapse, the honesty, the care I didn't expect—I finally felt ready. I started to talk about something I had never shared before: my relationship with food.

I told him about the days I wouldn't eat. The purging. The obsession. I told him how my parents thought I could just 'snap out of it,' how they didn't understand that it wasn't a choice. He listened closely. Then he said, "Kaylynne, what you're describing... this isn't just a phase. It's an eating disorder."

"No," I said immediately. I didn't want that label. I didn't want to believe it.

"There's no shame in this. You've been through trauma. This happens to a lot of survivors. Based on what you've shared, it sounds like you meet the criteria for an unspecified eating disorder."

"I can't have an eating disorder," I whispered. "My parents wouldn't understand."

I didn't run. I didn't lash out. I just sat there in silence, trying to make sense of it all. For weeks, I kept that diagnosis to myself. I tried to manage it alone. But the truth was, I didn't want to live like this anymore. Eventually, I opened up to my parents. My mom didn't know what to say. My dad thought I was choosing it. And that was the last time I brought it up to them. Mealtimes became battles. I couldn't explain what I needed, so I stopped trying. I kept my struggle hidden because saying the words "I have an eating disorder" still felt too heavy.

But behind closed doors, I fought to heal. I resisted the urges to restrict, to purge, to weigh myself, to stare into the mirror for hours. It wasn't perfect, and it wasn't quick. But it was something. Late one night, I messaged an old friend, Anna. We hadn't talked in a long time, but I just needed someone to hear me.

"I'm struggling," I wrote. "I was diagnosed with an eating disorder, and my parents don't get it."

She responded, "Wait, really? You don't look like you would have one—unless you've really changed." I stared at her words, reading them over and over. Then I blocked her and threw my phone to the floor. Her message echoed a fear I hadn't voiced: that my struggle wasn't valid because of how I looked. That I had to prove my pain.

I realized then that I only had one person in my corner: my psychiatrist. I told him that sometimes it felt like I had two voices in my head—mine and the eating disorder's. The disorder told me I wasn't enough unless I was thin, unless I was in control. But I had to learn to speak louder than that voice. I had to learn to speak for myself.

He encouraged me to join the eating disorder program after DBT, but I declined. Not because I didn't want help—but because I was scared. Scared of judgment. Scared of what my parents would think. But I kept working with him. Slowly. Steadily. And I started to realize something important: the eating disorder didn't define me. It was never who I was. It had become the only thing I could control, but it wasn't my identity.

I had been using it to cope, to bury trauma, to numb everything I didn't want to feel. But I was tired. Tired of fighting myself. Tired of feeling like I had to hide. And more than anything, I was tired of letting what happened to me dictate how I lived. I wasn't just made up of pain. I wasn't only what he did to me. He hurt my body, yes—but he didn't touch who I was. He didn't get to decide that. I did.

As summer 2020 gave way to a new year, I stood at the edge of something new. Not healed, but healing. Not whole, but rebuilding. The voices of fear were still there, but so was my voice. And for the first time, I was ready to use it. I wasn't just surviving anymore. I was beginning to fight for the life I deserved.

CHAPTER 23

Facing Fear

Over the course of three years, I worked hard to process the events that changed the course of my life. Even with the weight of trauma on my shoulders, I continued to chase my dreams in Taekwondo.

I pushed myself to be the best—earning gold medals and, at one point, even having once been featured in the news for my accomplishments. That happened before COVID, during a time when Taekwondo still felt like my lifeline.

Those moments were bright spots in a long, dark tunnel. But even with therapy—including exposure therapy—I realized there were still four obstacles standing in my way: my fear of men, my difficulty trusting people, the constant sense of being out of control, and the belief that my PTSD, eating disorder, and my battle with PNES might always define me.

And my biggest fear? That I wouldn't know how to protect myself if I ever felt vulnerable again—even with all my martial arts training. If my life were a Taekwondo tournament, then my fears were the final opponent standing between me and peace. I had trained for years, perfecting my kicks and punches. But what good was technique if I couldn't face what lived inside me? In Taekwondo, we're taught to face our opponents directly. In therapy, I learned the same thing: the way out is through.

I often repeated something a past therapist once told me: "Fear is a natural response to pain and uncertainty, but it doesn't have to control your life. When we choose to face the things that scare us, we create space for healing, resilience, and growth." I used that quote as a shield when fear hit hard. Still, I had to ask myself: Did I really want fear to walk beside me for the rest of my life? Fear had been a roommate in my mind for far too long. It was time to evict it.

In March 2021, I hit a breaking point. I was about to lose the support system I had relied on for over a year. My psychiatrist and I were nearing the end of our time together, and the fear of losing him made everything else feel heavier. Despite everything I had worked on in DBT, so many of my fears still lingered.

It felt like I'd spent three years climbing a mountain only to realize the peak was still far above me. But now, I see that those fears weren't failures—they were signs of what still needed my attention. Therapy taught me that healing wasn't just about moving on. I

It was about going inward, facing the pain, and finding a way forward. And for me, facing those fears wasn't just about healing—it was about hoping that, one day, my PNES seizures might stop too.

I knew fear was holding me back. It kept me scanning rooms, planning exits, and avoiding joy. I was trapped in 'what if' thinking—what if it happens again? What if I can't stop it? But nothing I had done so far had helped. I was tired of living in fear of the past, afraid of what might happen in the present or future. That fear wasn't protecting me—it was paralyzing me.

Eventually, I came across something online that stuck with me: *Fear is our body's built-in alarm system, meant to protect us from danger in the moment—but it was never designed to live in us forever.* The threat fades, but the memory can stay behind, echoing through our nervous system like it's still happening. And for me, that memory didn't just linger—it built a home in my body, quietly shaping how I moved through the world. It took strength to even recognize it, and even more to begin letting it go.

I made a decision that would shape every thing moving forward: I was done just getting through each day. I wanted to live—to feel the sun. To laugh without looking over my shoulder. To stop holding my breath. I realized that while I couldn't control the past, I could choose to stop reliving it every day.

Fear had shaped my story for too long. It tried to define me by a single chapter in my story: a teenager who had been raped. But I am so much more than that. My past had shaped me—but it didn't get to define me. I wasn't just one moment. I was every moment that followed it. The courage. The fight. The survival.

For years, I had confused safety with isolation. I thought avoiding people and staying guarded meant I was protecting myself. But in reality, I was just avoiding life. And I didn't want to keep doing that.

Most of my fears weren't about the past—they were about what *could* happen. But the worst had already happened. I had survived it. So why was I still living like danger was around every corner? I kept trying to close the door long after the threat had left.

I knew I had to move forward—not just for me, but for my parents, who never stopped fighting for me. And even for the people who didn't—those who stopped calling, who disappeared, who never showed up. The ones who knew what I went through but never asked how I was doing. To them, I say: *You didn't break me.*

But more than anything, I made a promise to live for *me.* Not out of anger, not to prove anything—but because I am worthy of a life beyond fear. I've crawled through the darkest places and fought like hell to be here. And now, I'm stepping forward—not as a victim of what happened, but as the author of what comes next.

Fear may still whisper sometimes, but it no longer gets to speak for me.

CHAPTER 24

Self-Love Through Ink

L ast year, my psychiatrist encouraged my family to help me switch schools—to get away from the place where I was hurt and into a space where my mental health would be understood. That's how I ended up in the Flex program in September. The Flex program was made for students who struggled to keep up in a typical classroom. Instead of strict deadlines, we were given all our assignments up front and could work through them at our own pace, either at home or at school.

That kind of flexibility made all the difference for me. I could take breaks when I needed to, and the teacher actually understood mental health. Most days, I worked from home, only going in when I needed help. It was a system that worked. I started the year with only one credit from Grade 9—and by March, I was nearly finished Grade 11.

On March 3rd, 2021, I decided to go in. My work was mostly done, but sometimes being at school helped distract me. I had been struggling with the question of whether or not my case would ever make it to court. I had stayed silent for so long, and I didn't know if there was enough evidence for anything to happen. The thought looped through my mind until I needed something to pull me out of it.

A notification popped up on my phone from an app I had been using to track my self-harm recovery. I opened it and saw the number: 1 year, 0 months, 0 days, and 42 seconds. That's how long it had been. A real smile lit up my face. I took a screenshot to save the moment, feeling proud without even realizing it. My teacher noticed.

She came over and sat beside me. "What's that smile for?" she asked kindly. I didn't say anything—I just showed her the screen. Her face lit up. "I am so proud of you," she said. "Can I give you a hug?" I nodded, and she wrapped me in the kind of hug that says, *I see you. I know how far you've come.* Just then, someone in the back of the class raised their hand with a question. My teacher glanced at them, then leaned toward me and whispered, "I'll be back."

"I'm actually going to go for a walk," I said. She knew walks helped me reset, so she nodded and reminded me to come back in 15 minutes. As I stepped outside, I called my mom. She answered, and before she could say anything, I blurted out, "Guess what? I'm one-year self-harm free!"

"That's amazing!" she said, and I could hear the relief and pride in her voice. We didn't talk long, but in that short moment, it felt like the weight of the past year had lifted just a little.

But as soon as I hung up, something shifted. The pride faded. I looked down at my left arm and saw the scars—reminders of everything I had been through. Just like that, the old shame crept back in. I returned to class, trying to distract myself by tapping a pencil against the desk. Soon it was time to leave. As I packed up, my teacher said, "Hey, I'm proud of you."

"Thank you," I replied with a small smile.

"If you want, you can head out a little early." She often did that when she sensed one of us was having a tough day. I grabbed my bag and headed outside.

My mom was waiting in the car. "I'm so proud of you," she said again, glancing over at me.

"Thanks," I said, but the truth was—I didn't feel proud. I couldn't explain it. I just didn't feel it. That night, I had an idea. One I assumed my parents would immediately say no to. But still, I couldn't shake it.

I walked into the living room. "Can I please get a tattoo to cover my scars?"

I braced for a hard no. But instead, my dad surprised me. "If you find something meaningful, your mom and I will think about it."

"Actually?" I asked. They knew how much the scars bothered me—how often I avoided short sleeves and how painful it was to answer questions about them.

My dad added, "Normally, we'd say no. But with what you've been through, if it's something you truly want, we'll consider it."

I smiled all the way back to my room. That night, I scrolled through Pinterest and Google, searching for something that wasn't just a design—but a message. I found it: a rose, with a stem that read: *love yourself*. I couldn't stop staring at it. For so long, I had hated my body, destroyed it, ignored it. But this—this tattoo meant something *love yourself*. The rose stood for strength and growth. It was a promise to myself that I wouldn't give up.

The next morning, I showed it to my parents. "That's pretty," my mom said softly. She didn't say much else. I think she was just worried I might regret it later. Neither of my parents had tattoos, so I knew this was completely new for them—something they'd never had to think about before. But they understood the meaning behind it.

A week later, on March 12th, we went to the tattoo shop. My dad signed the consent form since I was still underage. And then it happened—I got a rose tattooed over my scars, the stem engraved with *love yourself*. It wasn't just ink. It was healing. A permanent reminder that my past didn't have to define me. That I had one shot at this life, and I wanted to live it fully.

It felt empowering to wear something so meaningful on my skin before I even turned 18. What started as a victory over self-harm slowly became something even bigger.

That phrase—*love yourself*—grew with me. It became more than a reminder to stay away from self-harm. It became a call to care for my whole body. To nourish it. To treat it with compassion. As I started working toward recovery from my eating disorder, the tattoo took on new meaning. It reminded me to be kind to myself through the hardest moments. I began feeding myself not from guilt, but from self-respect. I no longer saw food as punishment or control—it became care.

My eating disorder was something I had carried quietly for a long time. While I had opened up about it in therapy, my family never really understood the depth of it. They thought it was something I could just stop, not realizing how much it had taken hold of my life. So, when it came to recovery, I did most of the work on my own. Even without full support, I drew strength from within. Through therapy, self-reflection, and relentless determination, I slowly began to loosen the grip it had on me.

Eventually, those thoughts stopped running my life. I found healthier ways to regain control—meditating, living in the moment, reconnecting with Taekwondo. I started to feel peace again. But as April 1st, 2021 approached, that peace felt fragile. That day would mark the end of DBT—and saying goodbye to the psychiatrist who helped me believe in healing again and a life worth living.

CHAPTER 25

The Last Session

The moment my eyes opened, I knew today would be different. A heavy knot tightened in my stomach as I remembered what lay ahead—my final session with the psychiatrist who had walked beside me through some of the darkest moments of my life. It didn't feel real. It felt like losing a safety net I had only just learned to trust. My heart pounded with a quiet fear: what would life look like without his support?

I forced myself out of bed and went through the motions of getting ready, but it all felt distant as if I were going through the motions of a life that wasn't truly mine. Every task felt overwhelming, my thoughts clouded with worry and doubt. As the appointment drew closer, a growing sense of fear and anxiety began to swell within me. What if I couldn't manage things on my own? What would happen if I slipped back into my old habits without his guidance?

The drive to my psychiatrist's office felt like a blur of anxious energy, the streets flashing by as I struggled to control the growing wave of fear. When my mom parked the car, we made our way toward his office, my steps stumbling slightly. Memories of our sessions together began flooding my mind. He was the one who had taught me how to rescue myself in times of crisis when I believed I was beyond help. His words had served as a beacon of light when I found myself drifting in the shadows of my own thoughts.

As I stepped into the hospital and made my way toward his office, the familiar scent of disinfectant filled the air. I approached the front desk, informed them of my arrival, and then sat down with my mom in the waiting room. My psychiatrist's office door loomed ahead—an unspoken barrier between me and the uncertain future that awaited.

A moment later, I was greeted by his warm smile as he led me to his office, leaving my mom to wait in the room behind. Sitting across from him, the silence between us grew heavy with unspoken emotions. The walls that had once kept my darkest thoughts at bay now felt like they were closing in on me. The weight of the journey hung in the air, a reminder of the struggles I had faced with his guidance at my side.

Halfway through our session, I reached into my bag and pulled out a thank-you card I had poured my heart into. I handed it to him without saying much, letting the words on the page speak for me. As he read, the silence in the room felt sacred—thick with emotion and years of healing between us. When he looked up, there was something in his eyes I'll never forget.

"You've come such a long way," he said, his voice steady and full of pride. "It's been an honour to witness that growth. The truth is, you did the hard work—I was just here to support you through it. You've built the strength to keep moving forward, even when it was hard to believe in yourself." Those words hit something deep inside me. He wasn't just saying goodbye—he was handing the strength back to me. "You're ready for this," he said. "You've already proven it to yourself."

As he finished reading, tears welled up in my eyes. I could tell he felt the weight of the journey we had shared. He set the card down gently, looked at me, and said,

"It's okay to feel scared about moving forward, but I want you to know—you're capable of continuing this work. You've done more than survive. You've rebuilt."

Then he added something I'll never forget: "I know how much you've struggled with suicidal thoughts, and I need you to remember this—your problems never required you to die in order to be solved. They needed your courage, your resilience, and you've shown all of that. You've proven time and again that you can face what once felt impossible."

I nodded slowly, letting his words sink in. He reminded me that although our regular sessions were ending, he was still available for monthly check-ins until I turned eighteen, which wasn't far off. He also told me that if anything good happened—or if I ever needed to share something—I could always send him an email. That meant a lot. I knew deep down this was a turning point. His guidance had helped me reach this place, but now, I had to continue the journey on my own.

But in the back of my mind, I knew this was the last day he could support me in the same way, as I would soon be transitioning back to my previous therapist, the one I had seen before starting DBT. However, one thing I had learned was that the people who grabbed your hand while you were drowning wouldn't always be there to save you. The only person who could truly save you is yourself.

As our session came to an end, I struggled to express my feelings of both gratitude and fear. I understood that this wouldn't be the last time we'd speak, but it was truly my final therapy session with him. He looked at me with a deep understanding in his eyes, quietly acknowledging the therapeutic relationship that had developed. I realized that he had given me the tools I needed to navigate the rough waters of my mental health journey.

As I stepped out of the office that day, an ocean of emotions exploded within me. Grief for the end of this phase in my healing journey, yet also a sense of accomplishment for the progress I had made. The path ahead of me was unclear, but as my mom drove off, I felt assured that I had the strength and resources he had given me to confront whatever challenges awaited.

Later that afternoon, not long after we got home, my mom's phone rang. She stepped into another room to take the call, and I sat quietly, already sensing what it might be about. When she returned, her face held a mix of emotion.

"I just got off the phone with Victim Services," she said. "They confirmed—your case is officially going to court." Her voice carried hope, and I felt it too. A quiet relief swept over me, knowing that my story mattered enough to be heard in front of a judge. There was finally enough evidence. But that relief quickly mixed with anxiety. What if they didn't believe me? What if my voice wasn't strong enough?

Still, I held on to what I'd learned: I had survived the unimaginable, rebuilt my life, and I wasn't the same girl who once believed no one would listen. This time, I was ready to speak up—for the truth, for myself, and for the justice I deserved.

Deep down, I was thankful my psychiatrist understood how hard it was to leave such a structured and supportive program. He didn't just let me go—he made sure I still had a lifeline. Knowing I could check in with him while preparing for the court case gave me a sense of stability. It reminded me that I wasn't facing this next step completely alone.

CHAPTER 26

From Panic To Purpose

The following day, I arrived at school and took my seat in class, hoping to escape my thoughts, but it felt impossible. My mind was spinning with memories—details I knew I'd have to recall for court. Then, without warning, a wave of panic crashed over me. My chest tightened, my breathing turned shallow, and I felt the overwhelming urge to escape.

I grabbed my bag and rushed into the hallway, tears spilling down my face. My teacher spotted me and followed. "Are you okay? Did something happen?" she asked gently.

I opened my mouth to answer, but the words caught in my throat. Just then, she noticed Mr. Adams, the school guidance counsellor, walking by. She called out to him, and when he saw me sitting on the floor with my knees pulled to my chest, he quickly knelt beside me. He spoke softly, but his voice barely reached me through the fog of panic. Over time, though, Mr. Adams had learned what helped and what didn't.

We had met many times to talk about the ways my trauma affected school. Unlike the school counsellor at my last school—who had dismissed my truth—Mr. Adams believed me. That changed everything.

He guided me through grounding techniques until we found what worked. One of the most effective was the 5-4-3-2-1 technique: five things I could see, four I could touch, three I could hear, two I could smell, and one I could taste. Slowly, my breathing would settle. Sometimes, he'd ask me to do it more than once until he saw the calm return to my eyes.

That day, once I was steady enough to stand, he walked me to his office. A group of girls kept staring as we passed, and he asked them—more than once—to give us space.

By the time we reached his office, my legs were numb, and my breath still felt shaky. I sat down, and he handed me a paper with a square printed on it.

"Let's try box breathing," he said. Using my finger, I traced the square—breathe in for four, hold for four, out for four, hold again.

"Do you know what triggered the panic?" he asked gently.

"Maybe," I mumbled. Eventually, I opened up about the stress of preparing for court.

He listened without rushing me. His calm presence made it easier to breathe. After I finished, he said, "Your past reflects what you've been through, but it doesn't define you. It's part of your story—but not the whole story."

I glanced at the floor and smiled slightly, then—like I always did when things got emotional—I changed the subject. "You know, with how good I've gotten at pretending everything's fine, maybe I missed my calling as an actress."

He smiled knowingly. "It's not healthy to hide your emotions," he said, "but I'll give you this—you're good at it. People who can do that might just make great actors."

"Maybe Hollywood missed out on their next star," I joked.

He raised an eyebrow. "You think I could really be an actor? I was kidding. You know I can't act."

He smiled, then shifted the conversation. "Kaylynne, you've been through more than most people can imagine. But let me ask—what do you want to do with your past?"

I looked around his office. A poster caught my eye. It said, "Mental health: Don't be ashamed to share your story. It will inspire others to speak up."

The words sank deep into me. I paused, then said something I hadn't fully realized until that moment: "I want to use my past to inspire others."

He nodded, the respect in his expression unmistakable. "Have you ever thought about sharing your story?" he asked. "Writing a book? Maybe even acting?"

"I don't know," I said quietly.

"You could change the world," he said. "Your story could change countless lives."

"Countless?" I asked, the word catching me off guard. I couldn't imagine how my story could ever reach that far, or make that kind of impact.

But something about the way he said it made me pause. His belief in me planted something I hadn't expected—hope. A sense of purpose.

I had written for years. Not with readers in mind, but to survive. My journal was where I went to untangle thoughts I couldn't say aloud. It held the secrets no one else knew. But as I reread the pages, I started writing with something else in mind—not just survival, but meaning. Maybe my story could actually help someone.

As I sifted through those pages, I came across a poem—one I had written not in a moment of victory, but in the raw aftermath of breaking down. It wasn't born from clarity, but from exhaustion. Yet within it, there was a quiet kind of power. That day, something shifted. I stopped seeing myself as what he had done to me and started seeing myself as what I had survived. I stopped calling myself a victim—and claimed the name survivor instead.

Survivor

Today, I made a decision. Not because the pain is gone. Not because what happened to me doesn't still echo in the corners of my mind. But because I'm tired. Tired of carrying shame that was never mine. Tired of letting his actions decide who I get to be.

Today, I stopped calling myself a victim. And I started calling myself a survivor. I didn't ask for this. I didn't deserve this. But I lived through it. And today, for the first time, I let that mean something.

I looked at my reflection and didn't turn away. I let the tears fall. I let the rage rise. And I didn't push it down or pretend I was okay. I just felt it. All of it. But I also felt something else— Strength. Not loud, not perfect. But real.

Because surviving isn't just breathing. It's choosing to keep going even when your body still remembers the moment it broke. It's picking up the pieces, day after day, when no one sees the effort it takes. It's learning to trust again—yourself, the world, your future.

Today, I said out loud: "What he did to me will not define me." And I meant it. I may still cry. I may still shake. I may still have days where the world feels unsafe.

But I survived. And now, I choose to live that way. Not quietly. Not ashamed. Not for anyone else's comfort. I survived rape. And I'm not hiding from that truth anymore.

I am a survivor. And today… is the first day I believe it.

CHAPTER 27

Preparation

On August 5th, my parents and I stepped into a building that loomed over us like a shadow—thirteen stories high, cold and intimidating. This was the place where I would begin preparing for the hardest day of my life. Across the street stood a beautiful brick courthouse, but all I could think was, *How many terrifying stories have been told in there? And how many were actually believed?*

We took the elevator to the sixth floor, which was dedicated to supporting victims of crimes like sexual violence and abuse. A woman greeted us with a warm smile as we entered. She had long blonde hair and thick glasses and introduced herself as Sarah, a Victim Advocate. She led us into a conference room, where another woman stood to greet us.

"I'm Emma," she said, shaking our hands. She was the attorney managing my case. I'd already spoken to Sarah on the phone a few days earlier, so seeing her in person felt slightly less intimidating. She looked at me gently and asked, "How are you doing, Kaylynne?"

I kept my head down, nervously playing with my hands. I couldn't get a single word out. Emma began the meeting by addressing both me and my parents. "We have a trial date—October 26," she said. "He's still pleading not guilty, which means it's going to move forward."

My parents immediately began asking a million questions—concern spilling out of them nonstop. I sat quietly, feeling myself start to detach.

Everything felt loud, overwhelming. It was like dissociation had taken over. After a few minutes, Sarah looked over at me and gently asked, "Would you be more comfortable if your parents stepped out for a bit?"

I nodded. Sarah turned to them and said, "Would you be okay stepping out for a moment so we can speak with Kaylynne alone?" My parents didn't hesitate. They nodded and stepped out. Once the door closed behind them, the room felt quieter. More focused. Like maybe now, I could finally speak.

"Now that it's just us, how are things at home and school?" Sarah asked.

I answered softly, "I changed schools this year. It was the best thing I could've done. I don't have to live in fear that he'll find me. School feels safe now. But at home... it's hard. My family's under a lot of stress. They're not really themselves."

Sarah nodded with empathy. "It's common for families to feel the weight of something like this. They care deeply. Sometimes they just don't know how to show it." Her words helped, a little. I smiled faintly. But in my head, questions kept spinning.

"Will I have to see him again? Will he be in the room?" I asked.

"Yes," Emma said gently. "But you won't have to look at him."

My stomach turned. "What if the judge doesn't believe me?"

"That's our job," Emma said firmly. "We believe you. That's why we're here."

She paused, then added, "This won't be easy, Kaylynne. If anything ever feels too much, you have to let us know right away."

"Alright," I whispered.

"And don't compare this to courtroom shows on TV," she said. "It's not like that." From my tone, it was clear they both understood I didn't want to be here. "In the upcoming weeks, we will take this time to help you prepare for your cross-examination, review your police statement, and address any questions you may have," Emma said.

Emma and Sarah both wanted to give me an overview of the courtroom where I would be sitting to provide my testimony, helping me feel a bit more comfortable. We exited the room and made our way through the waiting area where my parents were. Together, we all took the elevator to the second floor and then crossed a pedestrian overpass to reach the courthouse. We walked through a large area with doors lining the left side.

We reached one of the doors, and Emma opened it, inviting us in. The space was empty, with wooden benches arranged around an empty chair set up in a small cubicle, where Emma informed me that this would be my seat for the testimony.

"On that day, your parents can take a seat behind you."

"No," I quickly responded, cutting off Sarah. I couldn't bear the thought of my parents listening to the full details of my horrifying story.

"No problem. Some individuals might not find that helpful, and that's perfectly fine; they can simply wait outside the courtroom."

"I just want to go back home right now," I said.

"We've gone over a lot today, and I don't want to overwhelm you. If any questions come up or you need anything at all, please reach out. I'm here to support you," Sarah said softly.

That night, I barely slept. My mind was tangled with fear, anxiety, and the pressure of what was coming. And soon, it wasn't just my mind breaking down—it was my body too.

In the days and weeks that followed, my PNES seizures became more intense with a force I hadn't experienced in a long time. They were happening at home—sometimes out of nowhere—and it reminded me just how much trauma can live in the body, and how little control I had when it hit.

During court preparation, they became more frequent and more frightening. I would collapse on the floor at home, sometimes without warning. My body would shake uncontrollably. There were moments I couldn't speak or move, even though I was aware of what was happening around me. My parents were terrified. They began watching me more closely, especially when I spent time alone in my room. There were a few times they had to call 911 after I collapsed and hit my head during a seizure.

One night, I overheard my mom whisper to my dad, "I'm scared she's going to have one while testifying." That fear stuck with me—not just because of what she said, but because I knew it was real.

The seizures weren't just scary—they were dangerous. Not because they were life-threatening like epilepsy, but because they were PNES seizures—sudden, misunderstood, and still powerful enough to wreck me. They were trauma's way of making itself known, stealing control in an instant and leaving me to deal with the aftermath.

A deep fear lived in me—that I might break when it mattered most. What if I couldn't get the words out? What if my body gave out on me while I was trying to tell the truth? But I pushed through. Even when my body tried to betray me. Because I needed to do this. I needed to speak—for me, and for every other person he had hurt.

I tossed and turned that night, thinking about how many individuals remain silent about sexual violence, realizing that silence often feels like the easier choice.

I felt nervous about what lay ahead, yet my goal was simply not to seek complete justice for myself. I wanted to seek justice in order to advocate for numerous survivors and those whom Noah may have harmed. Eventually, I fell asleep.

As the weeks passed, my parents agreed to let me invite my friend Madison to our cabin for a much-needed escape. Being at the cabin with her felt like breathing again. We made inside jokes, spent time on the water, walked through nature, and stared at the stars like the world had paused just for us.

But that peace didn't last. One morning, my family decided to visit a small town about twenty minutes away with Madison and me. That weekend had been peaceful—Madison and I were finally able to laugh again, to breathe, to feel normal. But everything shifted during that short trip.

As we drove, my phone buzzed with a message from an unfamiliar account: "Hi." I ignored it at first, trying to stay in the moment. We walked around, grabbed food, and eventually returned to the car.

That's when I gave in and replied, "Hey, who is this?"

The response stopped everything: "Are we allowed to talk?" It was Noah. Panic surged through my body. My phone began buzzing nonstop with messages. "I've changed," he wrote. "I just want to be friends." Then came, "Let's leave the past behind and start a new chapter." And finally, "Forget the old one like it never happened." He denied everything, twisted the truth, and tried to rewrite our history. My entire body felt like it was shutting down. I showed Madison the texts. I couldn't speak. I couldn't believe what I was reading.

By the time we got back to the cabin, my parents could tell something was wrong. I hadn't said a word, and the look on my face said everything. The panic had already settled into my bones. I collapsed in my room, having a seizure as Madison stood by my side. She told my parents everything. That moment unravelled everything we had been holding together.

While we were still at the cabin, my parents and I contacted the police detective assigned to my case. We explained how Noah had reached out through social media—what he said, and how it violated the strict no-contact order already in place. The detective told us they would be speaking with him directly and that this could lead to consequences. Even though I was overwhelmed, hearing that gave me a small sense of protection—like someone else finally saw how wrong this was.

A couple of days after returning home, I had to meet with my attorney and Victim Advocate in person. We sat down to begin reviewing the police reports and prepare for what was ahead. One of the things we went through was the video of me sharing my story with the police for the first time. As it played, all I could see was a scared girl—unsure of what would happen next, unsure if anyone would believe her. I found myself in tears, struggling to keep watching. But I knew it was necessary. Reliving it wasn't easy, but it was part of fighting back.

The night before October 26, I couldn't function. I couldn't get my thoughts out clearly. My brain felt foggy, my heart heavy. There were dark circles under my eyes, and I didn't feel ready. I don't think I ever could have been. That night, my mom walked quietly into my room. She sat beside me on the bed and held something in her hand. "I have a gift for you," she said gently. She opened her palm to reveal a beautiful necklace, the words *I am strong* engraved in small lettering.

"I want you to hold this necklace tight tomorrow," she said. "I believe in you, and I know you can do this." I didn't feel strong. My body had been fighting me for weeks. My mind had been filled with fear. But in that moment, holding that necklace in my hand, I realized something: even if I broke down—shaking, crying, even collapsing—I was still showing up.

And maybe that's what strength really is.

CHAPTER 28

October 26th, 2021: The Trial

I woke up at 5 a.m., dragging myself out of bed just in time to nearly get sick in the toilet. I sat on the cool bathroom floor, resting my head against the seat, overwhelmed by nausea. At that moment, curling up beside a pile of my own vomit felt more bearable than walking into that courtroom. But eventually, I pulled myself together and returned to my bedroom.

The night before, I had carefully chosen my outfit: black dressy pants, a white tank top tucked in, and a black cardigan. But deep down, I wanted to wear sweats and a hoodie—something that would make me look as invisible and unapproachable as possible.

Emma hadn't told me what to wear, but my mom insisted I dress appropriately. I tried to put on a little makeup, but I ended up crying it all off.

"I'm not sure I can do this," I kept whispering to myself.

By 7 a.m., my mom came into my room to check on me. I was still sitting on the edge of my bed, tears pouring down my face. "It'll be okay," she said gently.

I handed her the necklace she had given me and asked, "Can you help me put this on?" She clipped it around my neck and gave me a reassuring smile.

About two hours later, we got in the car and drove to the building where I had spent so many hours preparing for this moment. All I could think was, *Just speak your truth. Trust the system.*

That thought echoed in my head as we stepped into the elevator and rode up to the 6th floor. When the doors opened, we stepped into a waiting area where Sarah met us.

She took a moment to check in with me and offer some reassurance before guiding us across to the courthouse. Once inside, she led us to a private room furnished with two couches and a window overlooking the city. The view was calm, almost comforting—nothing like the storm of emotions I was carrying inside.

While my parents spoke with Sarah, my attorney Emma walked in. She immediately noticed the stress on my face. "How are you feeling?" she asked.

"I don't know," I said. "I've been telling myself I'm a survivor, but today... I feel like a victim. To the court system, I'm just an 'alleged victim,' and I hate that label."

"Kaylynne, you are a survivor," Emma said softly. "You lived through something horrific. Today is about standing up for that truth."

"I am a survivor," I repeated quietly. I wasn't just some name in a file. I was a fighter, showing up for justice. Then Emma told us that Noah was already in the courtroom with his lawyer. Hearing that made my stomach twist. I tried to distract myself, but I couldn't focus. Eventually, Emma said she would head to the courtroom and return when it was time.

Sarah tried to make small talk, but I was lost in my own thoughts. Minutes passed. Then more. The silence stretched, heavy and tense. It felt like forever before there was finally a knock at the door. I knew it was Emma. She opened the door, and this time, her expression had changed. "Noah entered a plea deal. He's pleaded guilty to sexual assault," she said. "You won't have to testify."

My parents started asking questions, but I couldn't even process their words. I had spent months preparing myself to take the stand, and now—suddenly—I didn't have to. "What if I still want to testify?" I asked.

"You could, but I'd advise against it," Emma explained. "If a trial happened and the judge didn't find enough proof for a conviction, he might walk away with less accountability."

I was stunned. No one had told me a plea deal was even an option. I thought this was going to trial—everyone had made it sound like that was the only outcome. "He didn't just sexually assault me," I told Emma. "He raped me. He hit me. He did so much more."

Emma gently explained that even if he had pleaded guilty to more charges, the sentence wouldn't change because the assaults happened while he was still a minor. "This is the best possible legal outcome," she said.

I sat on the couch, numb with anger and confusion. I had spent so long preparing. As scared as I was, I felt ready. I was going to own that courtroom. But now it felt like my voice had been taken away.

Yes, I got what I wanted—a guilty plea and a sentencing—but I still wanted him to see me. I wanted him to know I hadn't forgotten a single thing he did to me. Eventually, I left the courthouse with Sarah and my parents. *I should feel relieved,* I thought. *But why don't I?*

Sarah walked us to the front doors. "I'll reach out when we have the sentencing date—it'll likely be sometime in the new year. But if you need anything before then, don't hesitate to contact me," she said. I smiled at her as we left, but inside, I felt empty. The drive home was silent. My parents reminded me that this was a good outcome, and I knew they were right—but it still wasn't what I had expected.

When we got home, I climbed into bed and pulled the covers over my head. I just wanted to disappear. But I couldn't stop thinking about him. He confessed to sexual assault—but I still saw him for what he was.

A rapist.

CHAPTER 29

The 10th And Final Time

The sun rose, and I don't think I had moved since coming home the day before. Did he always plan to plead guilty on the day of trial—dragging me through months of emotional prep—just to flip the script at the last second? Rage sat in my chest like fire.

When I finally rolled out of bed, I was numb. I glanced around my room, desperate to release the fury I had nowhere to put. After over a year of recovery, I was back in a place I never wanted to return to: the edge of a relapse.

Staring down at the harm I had caused myself, I whispered, "I feel like a fucking failure. A disappointment to myself and everyone around me." That hopelessness dragged me to the floor, where I sat behind my bedroom door, making sure my parents couldn't come in. I stared blankly at the wall until my eyes landed on a quote I'd taped up months before: "When you can't control what's happening, challenge yourself to control the way you respond to what's happening. That is the source of strength." —Tiny Buddha.

That quote made me pause. I didn't have control over his guilty plea, or how everything unfolded—but I did have control over how I treated my body. That realization hit hard. Thankfully, I had therapy that day. My new therapist knew that going to court would be difficult, so we had already scheduled a session. I left my room pretending everything was fine, trying to hide the damage beneath my sleeves.

But I wondered if I was doing a good job hiding it—if my mom could sense something was off. She asked in the car, "What's wrong?"

Was it the way I fidgeted? My bouncing knee? The way I gripped my sleeves in a fist to keep them from rolling up? I told her I was fine. We drove in silence.

When we got there, I slammed the car door behind me, rage still boiling inside. My mom definitely knew something was wrong then.

"How are you feeling after yesterday, Kaylynne?" my therapist asked gently, settling into his chair.

I didn't say anything. I just rolled up my sleeve and showed him the fresh marks. "I don't know—does this show you how I feel?"

His eyes softened. "I hope you're not blaming yourself for how you coped."

"Why wouldn't I? It's been over a year," I said, full of shame.

"Recovery isn't linear," he said. "Even after a year—or ten—it's still possible to relapse. That doesn't mean you failed. It doesn't erase how far you've come.

Recovery isn't about being perfect; it's about finding the strength to keep going, even when you fall. Can I ask about yesterday? How did it go?"

We talked about how Noah pleaded guilty. I told him, "It felt like he made me dig up everything I buried, just to never have to hear it."

He nodded. "Preparing for that day takes an incredible toll."

"And it's not like pleading guilty means I'm getting justice," I added. "He's not going to jail. He was a minor."

"I can see how heavy this feels," he said. "But your healing matters more than anything. Let's focus on what you need to stay grounded through this." I knew he meant well, but in that moment, the idea of moving forward felt impossible. I was exhausted—mentally, emotionally, physically. I wanted to lie in the wreckage.

Long before the trial, I knew I might have the chance to write a Victim Impact Statement—only if he pleaded guilty or was found guilty in court. I wanted to be ready. So I sat down one day, determined to start writing. I opened my laptop, stared at the blank screen, and tried to find the words. But nothing came. I had so much to say, and yet I couldn't begin. Now that he has pled guilty, I finally have the chance to speak—but I still don't know how to put into words the damage he caused me.

The trauma lived in my body. I wore long sleeves to hide bruises from hitting myself during panic attacks. Flashbacks triggered seizures and dissociation. I hated taking showers—touching my own skin felt revolting. Some days, I woke up feeling like I was trapped in a body I didn't want.

By November, I knew I was falling. The thoughts were heavy. I didn't know why they hit so hard—but they did. I didn't want to die. I wanted to be saved. But to survive, I had to do the one thing I feared most: admit myself to the psych ward.

On November 15, 2021, I checked in for the tenth time. A psychiatrist met with me, holding a thick binder of my history. "I see this is your tenth admission," he said. "I guess you're familiar with how this works." I just nodded.

We went through the usual intake questions, until he asked, "What are your dreams?" I didn't answer. I didn't have any. How could I, when I didn't even believe I had a future?

Four days in, it felt like dreaming was impossible. I paced my room, trying to quiet the urge to hurt myself. I looked through my things and found a notebook, some pens, and hidden inside my pencil case—something I hadn't seen in over a year. A blade. The nurses had missed it while checking through my belongings. I couldn't think. My body took over. I harmed myself—badly. When I saw the blood pooling beneath me, panic set in. "What the fuck did I do?" I cried out, frozen in fear.

A nurse rushed in. "I'm sorry!" I yelled. "I'm sorry!" The psych ward erupted into chaos. Nurses stripped the room, another tried to stop the bleeding.

A doctor came and said, "She needs stitches."

That night, I lay on the hospital bed as the doctor stitched my leg—twenty-four stitches in total. The pain was sharp, but it didn't compare to the shame burning inside me. I couldn't believe how far I'd fallen. The room was full of people trying to help, but I felt completely alone. Being placed on suicide watch made it even worse. Every move I made was monitored. I felt like a danger to myself. I felt like I had become everything I had promised myself I wouldn't be again. And in that moment, I hated myself for it.

In the morning, I sat in my room, checked every ten minutes. When a nurse brought my meds, I asked, "Can I call my mom?"

"After you take these," she said.

I swallowed the pills and called. My mom answered. "Mom, I'm sorry," I said, choking on the words.

"I can't talk right now," she replied. "I just need time to process."

"Are you still coming to visit?" I asked.

"No. I need time."

I hung up and ran to my room. *She hates me*, I thought. *I'm a disappointment.* A nurse came in and asked if I wanted to talk. I didn't—but I said yes. She sat beside me and started talking about the future.

"If you could do anything with your life," she asked, "what would it be?"

I shrugged. "Nothing. I'm failing at everything."

She looked at me gently. "I believe your story will change the world—sooner than you think."

I looked at the ground. "You're not the first person to say that. But look at me."

Still, she believed in me. And in that moment, it mattered. Her words stayed with me. My parents needed time to process what I had done to myself—time to come to terms with the pain I was in.

A few days later, when they finally began speaking to me again, I couldn't stop thinking about what the nurse had said: *Your story will make a difference.*

That tiny spark of belief turned into something more. Maybe all of this hadn't been for nothing. Maybe I could use it to help someone else. I pulled out my notebook—not to self-destruct, but to dream. I wrote a list of goals: write a memoir, become a public speaker, work in mental health. I wanted to be a voice for those who hadn't found theirs yet.

For the first time in a long time, I had a reason to live. And I wasn't letting go of it. Twelve days after walking into that psych ward, I walked out with hope. And I knew—this would be the last time I ever hurt myself.

Because I had finally started to believe in the girl who survived.

CHAPTER 30

Acceptance And Forgiveness

The ride home from the hospital was quiet, but it wasn't the kind of silence that brings comfort. It held tension—unspoken and heavy. My mom knew what I had done, and I could feel her sadness even though she didn't say a word. I kept my eyes low, avoiding the weight of her gaze. Still, something inside me had shifted. I wasn't returning home as the same broken version of myself. Somewhere in the wreckage, I had found a flicker of hope—a quiet determination to live differently than before.

When we got home, I went straight to my room. The walls that once felt safe now mirrored the storm still spinning inside me. I knew I was different now—stronger in some ways, more grounded in others. But those new pieces of me were tangled with shame. I kept thinking about what I'd done to my body in the hospital, wondering what my parents must be feeling. The guilt clung to me like fog. And yet, through it all, there was something else quietly rising—a flicker of hope sparked by the nurse who believed in me when I couldn't. She had helped me imagine that maybe my story wasn't over. Maybe I was just beginning again.

I sat in the corner of my room, eyes drifting toward the ceiling, my mind full of the dreams I had begun to build. They weren't just ways to escape reality anymore—they felt real, like something I could actually reach for. I still felt unsure, even unsettled, but beneath it all, there was a quiet drive pushing me to move forward.

Sunlight peeked through my curtains, warm and soft. I realized I couldn't stay locked in my room forever. I walked to the kitchen and let my dog out into the backyard. As I stepped outside, the cool morning air felt like a gentle reminder that healing was possible. For the first time in a while, the world felt open—like maybe it was waiting for me to take the next step. Each breath I took seemed to wash a little more of the weight away.

Then came the sound of sirens. Sharp. Loud. Triggering. In an instant, the sirens yanked me back—to the fear, the confusion, the day the doctors first mentioned PNES. That day, they sent in a psychiatrist, and though I don't remember much of what he said, one line stuck with me: "Anger is like holding a hot coal with the intent of throwing it—you're the one who gets burned." At the time, it didn't make sense. I didn't realize that by holding onto the anger, I was only hurting myself. I believed anger kept me protected—that it gave me power. But now I understood what he meant. Carrying that anger was exhausting, and the only one it punished was me.

I snapped out of the memory and called my dog back inside. I went to my room, grabbed my journal, and flipped through its pages—pages I had never reread. They held so much anger, pain, and hatred. As I read, I finally saw it clearly: how deeply that rage had rooted itself in me. How much space it took up. How much it cost. I had been trying to control my world ever since he took that control from me. That need for control became self-harm. It became an eating disorder. And it all came back to him.

I kept wondering—how does Noah live with himself? Does he even realize the destruction he left behind? For so long, I held onto my anger like a shield. It made me feel like I had some kind of control, like staying angry could stop the pain from getting any worse. The truth is I thought it was protecting me, but all it really did was trap me. He never felt the weight of it—I did.

By December, I found myself back in my therapist's office. The room was quiet, except for the low hum of background noise. I stared at him, until he broke the silence. "Have you ever thought about acceptance?" he asked.

I fidgeted. "Kind of," I said. "My psychiatrist in DBT talked about it. But I never really tried."

"Would you like to talk more about that?" he asked gently.

I clenched my hands, trying to stay calm. "I just don't get how acceptance is supposed to help. How do I accept what he did to me?"

He nodded, still calm. "Acceptance doesn't mean saying it was okay. It means acknowledging what happened so it doesn't control you anymore. It's about finding peace in the reality of the past, so you can create a new future."

Something shifted in me after that session. The idea of acceptance began to grow. It wasn't easy. It didn't happen overnight. But I realized: I couldn't keep running from the past. If I wanted to heal, I had to face it. Acceptance helped me let go of the weight I carried, especially the anger I held toward him. But that wasn't the end.

One day, while listening to a speaker in a PTSD support group online, I heard a woman share her story. She had been abused by her ex, and yet the word that kept coming up in her story wasn't anger— it was forgiveness. She said, "When you've been abused, it's easy to stay stuck in the pain. But true strength begins when you decide to stop carrying what they did. Forgiveness isn't about them—it's about setting yourself free."

That hit me hard. Acceptance brought me part of the way. But forgiveness—true forgiveness—would set me free. Forgiveness wasn't about letting him off the hook. It wasn't saying what he did was okay, or that the pain just disappeared. It was about choosing to free myself from the chains his actions had wrapped around me.

Forgiveness didn't mean forgetting. It meant acknowledging the damage and deciding not to let it own me anymore. It was a process—a decision I had to make again and again, not because he deserved it, but because I did. Holding onto that hatred felt like carrying a weight that was never mine to hold. True forgiveness was about cutting the cord that kept me tied to what he did—and finally allowing myself the peace he never gave me.

During therapy, I worked through what it meant to forgive. I learned that when I refused to accept or forgive, I hurt myself. It led to impulsive choices, anger, avoidance, and emotional numbness. The rape had left a scar I couldn't erase—but the aftermath? That part was mine to control.

I had already lost enough. I wasn't going to let him take anything more—not my voice, not my future, not another part of who I was. That day, I made a decision: I was going to accept what happened, and I was going to forgive. Not because he deserved forgiveness, but because I deserve peace. I didn't want to carry the weight of his actions any longer. Forgiveness wasn't weakness—it was me taking back control. It was freedom. And I was finally ready to claim it.

CHAPTER 31

Freedom

January 1, 2022, began bright and cold. Frost covered the outside of the window as I stood, lost in thought, watching the world awaken. The cuts on my body had faded, but the memories still lingered—reminders of a past I was determined to move beyond.

I remembered my darkest years. In 2018, I was drowning in the trauma of repeated sexual assaults. By 2019, I was marked by scars and suicidal thoughts. In 2020, the police saved me more than once from suicide. 2021, I had faced 23 ER visits, 11 nights in hospital beds, and over 10 suicide attempts. But this was not who I was anymore.

For 2022, my resolution was clear: to choose life. I promised myself that my past would no longer define me. I wasn't just surviving anymore—I was rebuilding. One breath, one step, one day at a time.

Taekwondo became my reset button—the one place where everything else faded, and I could reconnect with myself. Every movement had meaning. The focus it demanded left no room for fear or self-doubt. Sometimes, I'd catch my reflection in the window during class—mid-kick, mid-punch—and for a moment, I didn't just see someone trying to heal. I saw someone who already was.

Outside of Taekwondo, I discovered running. What used to feel like punishment turned into release. I wasn't running from pain—I was running toward freedom. Every footstep reminded me that I was still here, still fighting.

With time, the world around me began to feel different. I noticed small things—sunlight, quiet moments, and fresh air. I started forgiving myself. I embraced a version of me that was still healing but no longer hiding.

My goals shifted. I wanted to master new forms in Taekwondo, collect more gold medals, and chase Nationals.

But my vision reached beyond the mat. I dreamed of becoming an advocate for mental health, of writing a book that could help others feel less alone, and of building a future in the mental health field where I could support people the way I once needed support. I wasn't a victim. I was becoming a warrior—with purpose far bigger than myself.

"I am free," I whispered. And for once, I believed it. The scars were still there, but they no longer held power over me. I had learned it wasn't the past that defined us—but how we respond. I had hit rock bottom before, but now I was climbing higher.

Freedom, I realized, wasn't just about letting go of the past—it was about reclaiming who I truly was beneath the damage. It meant refusing to carry the labels my trauma tried to give me. It meant choosing strength over silence, hope over fear. I had walked through pain, but I didn't have to stay there. I could finally move forward—and that, to me, was freedom.

I made a plan. I listened to audiobooks on healing, wrote down my goals, and kept training with everything I had. Some days, the memories crept in, but I reminded myself: it's not what happened—it's how I choose to rise.

February came, and with it, a different kind of setback—one that struck at the core of what had been helping me heal. On February 5th, during training, my knee gave out. The pain was all too familiar.

This wasn't just an injury; it was a disruption to the progress I had made in Taekwondo, the one place that had become my escape.

An MRI confirmed what I feared: surgery was unavoidable. Suddenly, my freedom felt fragile. Taekwondo had been the space where I reclaimed my power. Now, it was being taken from me. But even with crutches beneath my arms, I reminded myself—I could still move forward.

I turned 18 on February 10th. That birthday meant everything. Three years earlier, I wasn't sure I'd make it. Back then, my birthday had been a day I didn't want to reach. But now, it symbolized survival. It was a reminder that I had endured. Soon after, I had my final scheduled Zoom meeting with the psychiatrist who had supported me for so long. Throughout my journey, he had offered me a virtual space once a month to check in and stay grounded. His words had often anchored me when I felt like I was drifting. Officially saying goodbye was harder than I expected. But deep down, I knew: I had found my footing. I wasn't sinking anymore. I was standing tall.

March 10th drew near, and I began writing my Victim Impact Statement. I had scribbled thoughts for months, but now I focused. It was hard. And being on crutches made it harder in a way I couldn't fully explain. Maybe it was the vulnerability, or the fear that he might see me physically struggling and think he still had power over me. Maybe it was just the reminder that my body was still healing in ways I didn't always want others to see. Whatever it was, it added another layer of emotion to an already painful process.

But I pushed through. I rewrote it again and again—pouring in every ounce of pain, strength, and truth. This was more than a statement. It was my voice. It was my story. It was my declaration that I was free.

Free from silence. Free from shame. Free from his control. When I closed my laptop, I knew: I had taken the first step toward closure. The next would be the hardest.

Facing him.

CHAPTER 32

Victim Impact Statement

March 10, 2022

I opened my eyes to the first light of morning, my heart pounding with nervousness. Today was the day—the day I would face Noah. The day I would read the most powerful thing I had ever written: my Victim Impact Statement.

I lay still for a moment, replaying the words in my mind, each one holding the weight of years I'd fought to survive.

I threw off the covers and swung my legs over the edge of the bed, immediately feeling the weight and stiffness of the heavy knee brace wrapped tightly around my leg.

The pain shot sharply through my knee, each throb a reminder of how far I'd come and how much this injury had taken from me. It was more than discomfort—it made me feel exposed, like my physical weakness might be seen as emotional weakness, too. But I wouldn't let that stop me.

I dressed slowly, carefully, ending up in the same clothes I had picked out when I thought I would be testifying months ago—clothes that reminded me of how far I'd come and helped me feel steady, not broken. Around my neck, I clasped the necklace my mom had given me—the one she gave me on the day I thought I'd have to testify. It was more than jewelry. It was a symbol of everything I'd survived to get here.

In the kitchen, my parents waited. Their faces carried both worry and a kind of quiet support that didn't need words. We didn't need to say much—our eyes exchanged everything we felt.

They had written their own Victim Impact Statements, choosing to submit their statements in writing rather than read them aloud in court. They had been given the option to speak, but chose not to.

They told me it wasn't because they didn't care—it was because they couldn't bring themselves to face the person who had hurt their daughter so deeply.

The idea of sitting in that room with him, trying to find words through the pain, was simply too much. And I understood that. Their pain wasn't separate from mine—it lived alongside it. But while they couldn't face him, I knew I had to. Even with the fear in my chest and the pain in my leg, I knew this was my moment to take back the power he had stolen. No matter how hard it was, I would not let fear silence me. Not this time.

I remembered the lines my parents had written: *November 2018 shattered our world, leaving us trapped in an endless nightmare. The aftermath changed our entire family. Our daughter's pain became our own. We lost laughter, peace, and normalcy. We sacrificed everything to support her.*

Those words echoed in my heart. My trauma hadn't been mine alone—it had stolen from all of us. I remembered the nights when I wasn't sure I'd survive, the moments when suicidal thoughts felt louder than my own voice. Through it all, my parents had stayed beside me, giving up so much to make sure I was never alone.

The drive to the courthouse blurred by in waves of tension. My hands fidgeted, adjusting my crutches as the throbbing in my knee throbbed with each turn. What would he think when he saw me like this? Would he even care? I tried not to let those questions overpower me, but they lingered just beneath the surface.

Arriving at the courthouse, I took a long breath. The air was cold, but it helped calm me. My parents stood close, silent but steady. We met with Sarah, my Victim Advocate—someone who had walked with me through every difficult part of this legal process. After a brief talk, we made our way across the pedestrian overpass toward the courtroom.

Emma, my attorney, was waiting for us, calm and composed as always, ready to guide us through what came next. She walked us through the possible outcomes, making it clear that she would fight for the maximum sentence allowed under youth court law. As we approached the courtroom doors, the reality of what was about to happen settled like a weight on my chest. When we stepped inside, it wasn't just a room—it was the place where I would reclaim my power.

My eyes scanned the space until they locked onto the podium where I would stand. And then, as if drawn by gravity, my gaze landed on him.

Noah.

He sat still in front of the judge, not looking around, not acknowledging my presence. But I saw him. And for a moment, I let myself feel everything—grief for the girl I used to be, rage for everything he had taken, and strength for how far I had come. Then something shifted inside me. For once, I didn't feel powerless in his presence. I felt in control. I wasn't here to ask for anything—I was here to speak the truth he had tried to silence. And in doing so, I was taking back everything he thought he'd stolen. This was no longer his moment. It was mine.

The judge entered and spoke briefly, outlining the purpose of the hearing and confirming Noah's presence in the courtroom. My parents sat beside me, silent but strong. Sarah sat behind me for support. Across the room, Noah had one person with him, seated separately on the other side. I could feel the weight of every breath, every glance. Then Emma looked at me and gave a slight nod. It was time.

Crutches beneath me, heart pounding, I rose. Sarah walked beside me, supporting me step by step until I reached the front of the courtroom. I paused at the podium. The quiet made everything louder—the sound of my breathing, the tremble in my hands. I took one final breath and looked up. Noah's head stayed down, unwilling to face me. But I faced him.

I stood tall. This was my moment. My truth. My freedom. And then I began to read.

Your Honour,
Standing here today, to be honest, I didn't think I'd be here to read about how this has affected my life, even though I feel it would give my power and voice back. It wasn't that I didn't want to read it because I knew it would be difficult; it was because I knew he would see me injured, the one person who shattered my life in pieces, the person who sexually assaulted me and made me feel weak, to begin with.

But I chose to be here today to read my Victim Impact Statement—given the fact that I knew he would see me injured and maybe looking weak but I'm not weak anymore because it took strength to get here today, and it took strength to live through what I've gone through and survive it all. For my whole life, I never thought that I would be standing in a courtroom—facing someone who sexually assaulted me and took my life away from me, but here I am today. November 2018 will forever be a date that is a memory that will forever be a scar.

Three years ago I would have never thought that my life would change in just one night, and I never thought that one person could cause this much damage to me, but was I ever wrong! November 2018 on a Friday evening is a time that a lot of people don't remember, but for me, I can't get that day out of my head. In so many ways I wish I could.

In fact, I would do anything to forget about the day where I was taken advantage of and was left traumatized and was shattered into billions of pieces. But I know there is nothing I can do to forget about that day. I spent the last 3 years cleaning up the mess I didn't make, but here I am today still cleaning the mess up. I have been on an emotional rollercoaster since day one and still am to this day.

I know right now there is so much I could say but I know nothing I will say will ever fully explain how much this has truly impacted my life. This is something that I will have to live with for my whole life and I know this is something that I will never forget. The only way to really understand the impact the sexual assault has had on my life is to understand the person I was before I was sexually assaulted.

Before I was sexually assaulted, I had so many dreams and goals in life that I wanted to accomplish. I always believed that my dreams and my goals would become reality someday. I was strong, confident, brave, happy, outgoing and I was also a very strong, fit and dedicated athlete. I had a strong passion for Taekwondo and I wanted to take that sport as far as I could, so I was training every day to become the best athlete I can. I was waking up early in the morning before school to train, training after school, going to Taekwondo 3 to 4 times a week and training on the weekends and I repeated that every day.

Slowly, my hard work and dedication were paying off. I was bringing home gold medals from tournaments and I knew I was heading towards the right direction to my dream, which was to make it to Nationals and I always had the dream to make it to the Olympics one day. Outside of Taekwondo, I also was going to school. I started high school in 2018 of the year I was sexually assaulted. I always worked very hard in school, did my homework and handed in all of the assignments that needed to be handed in and on top of that I would hardly miss any school from kindergarten to the time I was sexually assaulted.

At that point in my life before the sexual assault, I was really proud of myself—I was starting to go far in Taekwondo, my grades at school were the best they had ever been. I was right where I wanted to be in life. I really like who I became and I worked so hard to get to where I was and I knew I was heading towards the right direction in life but was I ever wrong! In fact, nothing could have prepared me for that Friday evening in November 2018, as my life fell apart right in front of my eyes. I really feel like my family and I went through hell and back all because of what happened to me.

To the person who I thought was a friend, ended up being someone who sexually assaulted me and who haunts me in my nightmares and who has emotionally broken me into a billion pieces and changed the person I used to be. He made me feel like an object more than a person and it makes me so extremely angry that someone had made me feel that way.

This crime has not just affected me in a small way—it has broken me, destroyed me and has torn me apart and left me feeling guilty, ashamed and powerless. The happy, positive, outgoing person I used to be was no longer me. I felt alone, unable to trust anyone and didn't even trust myself. After I was sexually assaulted I wasn't sure what actually had happened, but what I did know was the physical and emotional pain I had felt was the worst pain I had felt in my whole life. The shame I had felt was so overwhelming and the self-blame and self-doubt kept me from telling anyone.

For a year and a half, I kept it to myself. I had sleepless nights and there were many nights I stayed up rocking myself back and forth with the lights on because I was so afraid—afraid of having another terrifying and very disturbing nightmare. I dreamed that it was happening all over again and sometimes I was watching it happen right in front of my eyes, and I couldn't do anything about it. Soon I would wake up from the dream feeling fear and so much more, because of the dream I would tell myself it was just a dream but the thing is it wasn't 'just a dream.'

Sometimes when I would wake up I would think he was in my room; sometimes I would even hear his voice telling me that he would hurt me all over again, which caused so much fear. Sometimes I felt so scared to even go to sleep by myself. I also was experiencing very bad flashbacks almost on a daily basis making me relive that day all over again. I felt his hands touching me and I felt pain where he hurt me, and saw and heard everything that happened to me during every flashback I had.

On okay days they may last for only a few seconds, but on bad days they feel like they go on for hours on end, and are as physically and emotionally painful as the real event. I also had very bad panic attacks from the trauma and I was constantly dissociating—making me feel like I'm not here. Some days, I wouldn't even know what month it was or what day it was because I was dissociating so much, which was just a way of my brain trying to cope with the trauma.

I was constantly getting triggered by the smallest things, like going to pools or even the smell of pools, someone who raised their voice, arguments, bangs, physical touch, someone standing too close and I could name so much more. Everywhere I went I felt as if I was getting triggered by something, and it would lead into a flashback, panic attack, bad memories or sometimes I would dissociate. I was put on many medications to hopefully help me with all that, like helping me sleep at night, my PTSD, depression, anxiety and nightmares but medications don't make everything better—some days they feel like they do nothing.

I was exhausted 24/7 and I found it so difficult to even keep my eyes open. On top of that, I lost my passion for Taekwondo.

I was hardly going to school and I was isolating myself from family and friends. I was no longer the hardworking and dedicated person I used to be; I started to feel as if I didn't know who I was anymore. It felt as if I was in a dream but I couldn't wake up from it. I was living in my worst nightmare.

I remember I went from trusting others to someone who started to never feel safe around people. I remember being afraid of every guy who was in my life, and that included my own dad, who loves me and who would never do anything that would hurt me.

I even remember when I sat in school, I needed to be able to see everyone around me. I needed to know where each person was and what they were doing because that was how badly I didn't trust anyone.

I was paying more attention to what everyone else was doing around me, than what the teacher was teaching. I heard every pencil that was tapping, every clock that was ticking. I was aware of every knee that was bouncing and every phone that was out. I think I learned more about the students in my class than what the teacher was teaching. I went from someone who liked to be around people and to socialize, to someone who is scared of big crowds and is terrified when people get too close.

I remember I went from someone smiling at others on the street to someone who is now scared to walk down the street because everywhere I go I feel like I see him. Every person I see, every shadow I see, even every noise I hear—I think it's him, I just fear that one day I might run into him again.

All I wanted to do was stay home and hide; but being at home I still didn't feel safe. Him knowing where I live has made me feel sick to my stomach still to this day.

From the time when I was sexually assaulted, to a year later was probably the hardest time in my life as every day felt harder and harder to live. I started to have thoughts about suicide a week after I was assaulted; simply because I felt if I killed myself, I wouldn't have to remember what happened to me. I felt as though death would be no different than being alive. I just wanted all the pain to stop.

I was also self-harming to cope with the trauma that I went through, but all of the cuts on my body made me feel so ashamed and all of the scars that are now left on my body are just a reminder of what happened to me.

I couldn't look at myself in the mirror for the longest time because the person who was looking back at me, I didn't recognize. I didn't recognize that person who had cuts and scars down her body but I slowly realized that was me and when I realized that, I couldn't stop crying. I had many days where I would stand in front of the mirror crying because I felt so disgusted to be in my own body. Disgusted, knowing that someone went inside me without my consent. Sometimes I felt so disgusted to the point where I didn't want to be in my body at all. There were nights I thought about killing myself.

One year after the assault took place, I was hospitalized multiple times during that time for mental health. I also had three suicide

161

attempts because I didn't know how to live with the pain that came from the trauma, but the many hospital stays and the suicide attempts were not my last as I had many more after that.

The sexual assault wasn't the only thing that hurt me. Seeing my relationship with my parents change, and seeing my parents' mental health be affected as well, hurt me. The overwhelming guilt I felt for making my parents feel that way affected me.

Looking back now I had no reason to feel guilty because I had done absolutely nothing wrong. The trauma from the sexual assault I went through did not just affect me, it has affected everyone who is close to me, and that caused so much pain to me. I watched my parents, who I love, change. I wasn't the only one who was shattered into billions of pieces—my whole family was!

A year and a half after the assault was when I found the strength to no longer keep this as a secret and I was no longer going to keep this buried deep inside me because I needed something back that was stolen from me—my power. The only way I knew I would get my power back was to take responsibility for something that should never have happened to me, so I needed to do what was right. So I found the strength to do what was right for me, make a police report.

Reporting the sexual assault, I thought would help me get over this; but no, it didn't. In fact, it caused me more pain, and I had to relive what had happened to me all over again. I felt more ashamed than ever. A week after making the police report I ended up in the emergency room because I had a seizure. I was given medication to hopefully stop the seizure but nothing was working. I was put in a children's hospital for 7 days with my parents by my side.

After several tests were done, I was diagnosed with PNES—psychogenic nonepileptic seizures—which were caused because of the trauma from the sexual assault. Hearing that, I was absolutely devastated—especially finding out that there is no medication to stop these seizures.

The only thing they say that might work is therapy. which I have been doing since almost 2 months after the assault, and still am to this *day. Therapy is never a quick fix so I had to just learn how to live with something that I really shouldn't have to live with.*

Sometimes my seizures can last up to 2 hours long at a time and there have been times I bit my lip to the point where I almost needed stitches and I hit my head many times, where I ended up getting a bump on my head and sometimes even getting a concussion. There were times I was rushed to the hospital by an ambulance multiple times all because of the seizures, which were caused by the trauma I went through. I was emotionally drained and exhausted.

I didn't know how to live anymore, as every day I kept remembering what caused all this. On top of all that, I was waiting to find out if there was enough evidence for it to go to court—also waiting to see if anyone believed me. After months of making the report, I finally got the phone call that I had been waiting for.

October 26 was the day of court—the day I was supposed to testify. I woke up and I didn't want to go because I knew it was going to be hard, but I got out of bed, got ready and left the house because I knew it was the right thing to do, and I wanted to do the right thing even if it was the most difficult thing I would be doing.

But later I found out I didn't have to testify. Hearing that I didn't have to go in front of a judge and relive every moment of the sexual assault in horrifying detail, I had a sense of relief, but I was also angry. Angry, because I had to prepare for that day and none of it was easy. No matter how many times I tell myself this is going to be hard and I just have to deal with it. Nothing could have prepared me for just how painful it was just to prepare for the day of court.

When I left I thought that finally, finally, I could get on with my life. That this awful chapter in my life was over at last but I was wrong.

This is something that I will never forget, and I mean never. Almost a month after court I ended up staying in the hospital almost for two weeks with 22 stitches in my leg because of self- harm. Because of the sexual assault, I had 11 hospital stays and countless emergency room *visits, because of suicide attempts, self-harm and because of my PTSD from the trauma.*

There were times where my PTSD got so bad—to the point where the paramedics had to take me to the hospital or sometimes the police had to save me before I tried to end my life. I was then taken to the hospital where I was admitted to the psych ward—sometimes more than 10 days away from my family.

I also had to go to countless therapy appointments to recover from something that shouldn't have happened to me. I had countless intense therapy for me to try and recover from the assault and I am still doing therapy to this day. Therapy, to me, is something that I don't want to do, but it's something I have to do in hopes that someday—just someday—I will see my old self. The one who had so much confidence and who had a bright future ahead of her, with so many possibilities in life.

*Three years after the sexual assault, I am still heavily affected by this. Ask anyone close to me and they'll tell you that the past 3 years have been absolutely hell for me. I still struggle to live in my own body, as he made my body feel like an unsafe place to live. I can never seem to feel clean; every day I just want to get out of my own body, but there is nowhere else I can go. Since the assault, my brain has been at war with my body—constantly telling me **I'm in danger** just because I'm living in a body that went through something truly terrible.*

Some moments I know that I'm safe, other moments I feel I'm drowning in fear and pain. Most of the time, though, it's both. My body tells me I'm safe and my brain is screaming at me that I'm in danger and won't ever survive, For the past 3 years, all of my relationships have been affected by this. Many people close to me used to not know how to respond to what I've been through, but for the people who stood by my side, I didn't make it easy for them. I'm overwhelmed by the fear that they see me differently. I don't feel like a whole person; I feel like a sexual assault victim. I assume that people see me the way I see myself—dirty, disgusting, not clean, ashamed, worthless and so much more.

I feel like people don't see me how they used to see me; they see what happened to me, and that can hurt, because I know I am so much more than what happened to me. There have been countless number of days where I have woken up wanting all of this to be over. The best way I can describe it's like being trapped in a room and every time I thought I was close to finding a way out, the walls would start moving in. I lived in a state of panic because I thought if the walls moved in anymore, I would be crushed under the pressure of it all.

Standing here today, I never thought in my whole life that I would be standing in a courtroom—facing someone who sexually assaulted me and took my life away from me. I was just like everyone else, thinking my worst nightmare would never come true. When it did, I never thought I would have the strength to be here today. November 2018 will forever be a date that is a memory that will forever be a scar. On that day, I became a victim.

But today, I stand here as a survivor—a survivor who is fighting to get her voice and power back. The one thing I know about the past is it can never be changed. I wish I could because I would have never walked out of my house that day, but that is something I can't change. But what I do know is the future ahead is something you can change. So for you, Noah, I ask that you make a positive impact in every life you touch because the many negative impacts you made in mine and my families are enough for a lifetime. I ask you to take seconds, minutes, hours and days, to truly realize how the first time you laid hands on me, that Friday evening changed me from being a dedicated, strong athlete and a hardworking high school student to a victim, to a survivor. You know what happened in November 2018 on a Friday evening. You know and I know; and you can't erase that.

Most importantly, remember that you are paying the price of your own choices, while I have to pay the price of a choice that you did not give me. I never wanted to forgive you. However, holding onto unforgiveness felt like I was consuming poison while waiting for you to die. I had to forgive you—not for you, but for me. I want you to know that even though you broke me, destroyed me and tore me apart in so many ways that I will never forget, I will never let you rise above me because today, I got my power back, the power you stole from me.

As I finished speaking, the courtroom fell silent. Not the kind of silence that feels empty—but the kind that echoes with power. I stood there, heart pounding, my body trembling, yet something inside me had never felt stronger. I had read the most powerful words I'd ever written. I had spilled years of pain, shame, rage, and resilience into that courtroom—and I faced the one person who once tried to destroy me. But this time, he couldn't take anything. Because in that moment, I owned the room. I owned my voice. And I took back the power he had stolen.

My heart raced as I returned to my seat beside my parents. Their arms wrapped around me, grounding me. Their eyes welled with tears—not just from sadness, but from pride. They had watched me fall and rise, time and time again. They had seen every breakdown, every fight to keep going, and now—they watched me stand in a courtroom and reclaim my voice. They saw me fight for my truth, and this time, they saw me win.

Then the judge turned to Noah and asked, "Do you have anything to say to the Venn family?"

He stood slowly, eyes still looking down. "I have anger issues," he muttered, barely speaking above a whisper. That was it. No apology. No ownership. Just a weak excuse that didn't come close to showing he understood what he had done. His words vanished into the silence—empty, useless, and far too small for the damage he caused.

The judge looked at my parents and me, her tone shifting with empathy. "To the Venns," she said gently, "what you've been through is deeply painful. I'm truly sorry for everything this has put your family through. No one deserves to carry that kind of hurt."

Then she addressed me directly, her words landing like an anchor in my heart. "It's incredibly powerful when survivors like you choose to come forward and read their Victim Impact Statements. Your bravery and resilience are truly inspiring. Speaking your pain aloud in front of the person who caused it—that takes courage. And I want to acknowledge that."

I swallowed hard. In that moment, I felt it—I was seen. I was heard. I was believed. Her words didn't undo the trauma, but they gave something back to me I hadn't realized I needed: validation. As I sat there, Emma and Noah's lawyer began discussing sentencing. That's when his lawyer spoke again, cutting through the air with a suggestion that made my stomach turn. "My client can write a letter of apology to the victim," he said.

I felt my body stiffen. A letter? As if an apology scribbled in ink could erase what he'd done to me. I looked at Emma, and before I could even say anything, she stood up. Her voice was calm but firm, reminding the court that no letter could undo the impact of his actions. She spoke for me with strength and clarity, making it clear that this wasn't about words on paper—it was about justice. Watching her speak made me feel protected, like I wasn't standing alone.

The judge delivered the sentence: 18 months of probation, 3 months of community service, 2 years of counselling, and a strict no-contact order. It was the maximum allowed under youth sentencing. It was something. But it would never feel like enough.

Still, I held onto what mattered most. The judge believed me. She acknowledged the weight of his actions—even though she didn't know the full truth of what he'd done, because I wasn't allowed to speak about anything beyond the charge of sexual assault.

I couldn't talk about the hitting, the rape, the emotional abuse— or the time he pulled out a needle filled with some kind of drug. All of that remained locked inside me. But even so, she saw something in my eyes—something unshakable—and that gave me something the sentence never could.

But even more than that—what mattered most to me was that I stood in front of the person who had once destroyed me. I stood tall, strong, and whole. Every piece he tried to break, every part of me he thought was gone—I carried it up to that podium, pieced back together. I spoke my truth, and in doing so, I proved that no matter how hard he tried to silence me, he failed. I was whole. I was powerful. And I was free.

I thought about everything I had written—the hours I spent curled up in my bedroom, pouring my story into words, hoping it would be enough. And it was. Because that day, I didn't just speak—I rose. I took everything he tried to break and turned it into something unshakable.

I was no longer the girl he shattered—I was the woman who stood, unshaken, in the ruins and built herself back. I wasn't just surviving anymore. I was living proof that he didn't win.

CHAPTER 33

My Time To Rise

The next morning, I sat quietly in the living room, the early light casting soft shadows across the walls. The events of the day before still lingered heavily in my chest, but it wasn't the sentencing that echoed through me—it was my words. My Victim Impact Statement played on repeat in my mind, louder than anything the judge had said, more powerful than the punishment itself.

It wasn't just a statement—it was a turning point. Each word had broken chains I didn't realize I still carried. For the first time, I didn't feel like I was begging to be heard. I was speaking because I knew I mattered. The courtroom didn't define my story—I did.

As the quiet morning unfolded, I found myself doing something simple—grabbing a sweater, picking up my phone, letting the silence settle. Life was resuming, yet something inside me had deeply changed. It wasn't about sentencing or closure anymore. It was about reclaiming my space in the world. Not because the system validated me, but because I had validated myself. Facing him wasn't the moment I healed. It was the moment I remembered that my healing had already begun—and it was mine to continue.

Still, I knew the journey wasn't over. Healing was never one moment. It was made up of hundreds. Thousands. Some big, some small. This was just the next step. The days began to blend together. I spent hours in reflection, caught in the push and pull of relief, anger, sadness, and uncertainty. There were moments when I felt completely still, and others when the chaos felt like it might drown me. But through it all, one thing stayed steady: I wasn't where I used to be.

One afternoon, while sitting downstairs lost in the rhythm of music, the phone rang. I answered, hoping it was the call I'd been waiting on—and it was. My therapist had placed me on the waitlist for an adult therapy program before my 18th birthday. Now, I was officially enrolled.

The fear came quickly. I was no longer a youth. What if things were different now? Would I be dismissed or treated like just another adult in a broken system? Would they see me as someone too complicated to help, or someone too strong to need support?

The program ran Monday through Friday: daily group therapy, weekly individual sessions, and a structure that spanned five weeks. As it began, I noticed something unexpected. The skills we covered— grounding, mindfulness, emotional regulation—they were familiar. I had seen them before. I had used them before. I had lived them.

That realization was powerful. I already had the tools. I didn't need to be taught how to survive anymore—I just had to trust myself. I remembered something my psychiatrist once said to me during DBT: "I bet in ten years from now, things will be different." I didn't believe him then. But maybe, just maybe, he was right.

My weekly one-on-one sessions were helpful, but surface-level. We didn't go as deep as I used to. And that was okay. Maybe I didn't need to dig as much anymore. Maybe I was learning how to stand on my own. For years, therapy had been my lifeline. My safety net. But now, I started asking myself a new question: what if I was ready to let go of the net?

I began to notice a quiet but powerful shift within myself. When challenges came, I didn't spiral—I paused, breathed, and grounded myself. I recognized the tension in my shoulders, the racing thoughts, the signs of anxiety trying to creep back in.

Sometimes, memories of the past—of assaults, of hospitals, of the moments I thought I'd never survive—still surfaced. But they no longer controlled me. I had learned to respond differently. I was no longer stuck in the patterns of my past—I was present, aware, and evolving.

That self-awareness led me to ask a new question: Did I still need antidepressants? For four years, they had helped steady me through the storm. But just as I had grown beyond needing therapy every week, I wondered if I had also outgrown my dependence on medication. Could I continue healing without it? Could I stand fully on my own?

Sitting cross-legged on my bed, journal open, I flipped through page after page filled with years of emotion. Scribbled entries told a story of survival, yes—but more than that, of transformation. There were nights filled with tears, days filled with small victories, and moments of strength carved from chaos. My scars weren't weakness. They were evidence of a life I had fought for.

I saw the change. Where there had once been constant crisis, there was now calm. Where pain had once screamed, peace had begun to speak. With that clarity, I brought the question to my doctor. We talked openly, weighing the decision carefully.

And slowly, the fear that had once gripped me loosened its hold. Letting go of the medication didn't mean erasing what had helped me. It meant acknowledging that I had reached a place where I could keep going without it.

Antidepressants had been my bridge. But now, I could walk without them. That decision wasn't about control—it was about freedom.

In that moment, I realized: I had crossed into something new. I had faced darkness, walked through fire, and emerged not just standing, but rising. I had done the work, and it showed—not just in the absence of chaos, but in the quiet strength I carried. Surrounded by the same four walls that had once witnessed my lowest points, I felt something different: peace. The kind that doesn't erase the past but gently says, 'You don't live there anymore.'

Some days, the pain still whispered. But I had learned how to listen without losing myself. Healing wasn't perfect. It wasn't linear. But it was happening.

And I was living it. I had stopped measuring strength by how little I struggled. I started measuring it by how often I got back up.

And in the quiet of that realization, one truth became clear: The day I chose to rise—was the day I truly began to live.

CHAPTER 34

The Voice I Fought For

My journey has taught me that survival is just the beginning. It's the first breath after drowning, the first step after falling. But it's the moments that follow—the decision to rise, to heal, to speak—that truly define us. For me, those moments have been both brutal and beautiful, a dance between darkness and light.

Looking back, I remember how silence nearly destroyed me. But it also pushed me. The moment I chose to speak out was the moment I chose to live. I refused to let my rapist, the world, or even my own fear keep me quiet. I found my voice—and with it, I found my strength.

The path to reclaiming my voice wasn't easy. It was layered with shame, fear, and self-doubt. But with each step forward, I found resilience and a deeper sense of purpose. I learned that vulnerability is not weakness; it's one of the bravest things we can offer. My scars, both seen and unseen, became proof of that bravery. I came to see that my voice wasn't just something I reclaimed—it was something powerful I had all along.

Everything changed when I chose to turn pain into purpose. I took the darkest moments of my life and used them to build something meaningful. The trauma, the shame, the fear—they became the fuel that lit the path forward. Volunteering with Kids Help Phone allowed me to connect with youth facing battles I knew too well. I didn't just see pain in their stories—I saw fighters, survivors, and strength even when they couldn't.

In 2023 I went to college to start my career in the mental health field and I pushed myself through studies, something that once felt out of reach in high school.

By that time, the flashbacks and nightmares had finally faded. I still had good days and bad ones, but I was driven by a goal: to graduate with honours. I stayed up late studying, gave every assignment my all, and pushed through even on the hardest days. But what I achieved was more than I had imagined—I graduated with honours and was awarded Student of the Year. It wasn't just about grades; it was about proving to myself how far I'd come and honouring every quiet battle I had fought to get there.

After graduation, I was offered a job—one I never imagined I'd be strong enough to take: I was hired at the very place that once held me at my lowest—the Crisis Stabilization Unit.

I remember sitting there years ago, unsure if I'd make it through another day, buried under silence and pain. Now, I return to the same space, not as someone in crisis, but as someone who helps others find their way back to hope.

The same rooms where I once sat during some of my lowest moments are now places where I offer support, encouragement, and understanding. It's in those moments—when I get to offer someone compassion, to sit beside them in their pain without judgment—that I'm reminded why I do this work. Because everyone deserves to feel seen, supported, and not alone in their fight to keep going.

Some days, I glance at the intake door and remember the girl who walked through it, tears in her eyes and exhausted. Now, I sit on the other side of that door, offering hope to those who think they have none. That's the beauty of this journey: healing doesn't just pull you from the fire—it hands you the strength to walk back in and carry someone else out.

Writing this book became more than just a personal outlet—it became a turning point. These pages hold not only my story, but the strength I fought to reclaim. Each word I wrote was a way of standing up to the silence, a way of rewriting the narrative I once thought would break me.

Writing gave me something back when everything felt taken from me. It gave me power, clarity, and now—connection. Through this book, I'm reaching those who still feel lost, reminding them they're never alone in their fight.

So many people feel trapped by pain, but I need you to know—you can rise. You can fight. You can reclaim your voice. I wrote this book because silence is deadly. I wrote it because I once believed I wouldn't survive. I wrote it because every survivor deserves to be heard, seen, and believed.

We hear the term 'sexual violence,' but few truly understand its aftermath—the PTSD, the self-doubt, the shame. That's why I wrote this. To show not just the hurt, but the hope. To prove that even when it feels impossible, healing can happen. Today, I celebrate over three years without self-harm or hospital stays. The trauma is still part of my story, but it no longer owns me.

My body carries scars, some visible, some not. For a long time, I felt ashamed of them. But now I understand—each one is a chapter of survival. I may not be proud of what caused them, but I'm proud of the person I became because I kept going.

I owe so much to those who stood by me, who reminded me of my worth when I forgot it. To those people—thank you. You believed in me when I couldn't believe in myself.

Society tried to silence me—with its judgment, its harmful beliefs. But I refused to be buried. I chose to rise. I am no longer afraid of my story. I am no longer ashamed.

As I close this chapter, I no longer define my story by the pain I endured, but by the fire I walked through to reclaim my life. Strength wasn't something I found in peace—it was something I earned in the middle of the storm. And if you're still fighting your way out, please remember this: your voice isn't gone. It's waiting—for the moment you're ready to speak, to fight, and to rise.

Let my story be a reminder that healing is possible, that light can return, and that you are never alone. This is not just my ending—this is my beginning.

A Letter To My Survivors

To the one holding this book, If you've made it to the final page, it means you've walked alongside me through the darkest and brightest parts of my story. And now, I want to speak directly to you—especially if you're a survivor.

Maybe your case never went to trial. Maybe it was dismissed, ignored, or never even reported. Maybe you're still carrying the weight of what happened in silence. If so, I want you to hear this loud and clear: that does not make your voice any less powerful. That does not make your pain any less valid. And that does not make you any less of a fighter.

I found a piece of my voice the day I stood in court and read my Victim Impact Statement. But you don't need a courtroom to find yours. Your voice was never meant to be tied to a judge's ruling, a jury's decision, or a trial's outcome. Your voice is yours—it always has been.

You have the right to speak. To shout. To whisper. To write. To be silent until you're ready. Your healing, your journey, your pace—it's all yours to decide. Whether you share your story or guard it quietly in your heart, know this: you are already surviving in ways the world may never see, and that alone is something to be proud of.

Please don't let what didn't happen take away what still can.

You are not what was done to you. You are what you choose to do with it.

Keep going. Keep fighting. Keep finding your way—on your terms, in your time.

With all my strength and belief in you,

Kaylynne

Acknowledgements

I have been fortunate to have an incredible support system through-out my journey, and I am forever grateful. *Speak Up and Fight* would not have been possible without the help of the many wonderful people who stood by me.

To my readers, thank you for bravely engaging with my story. Your willingness to bear witness to my experiences means the world to me. I hope that my words made an impact on you and that you have found comfort in knowing you are not alone.

To my parents, with all my heart, I thank you. Your unwaver-ing love, support, and encouragement have been my anchor during the most difficult moments in life. You have stood by me through every storm, every breakdown, and every moment of doubt. Your presence has reminded me that I am not alone and that I am loved beyond measure.

To my family members who have chosen to stand by me, I thank you for your love and encouragement. Your support has been invalu-able, and I cherish the memories we've shared.

I also acknowledge those family members who chose to walk away because of my mental health and never reached out once to see if I was okay. Your absence has taught me the value of resilience, self-reliance, and the importance of surrounding myself with people who support me.

The journey through the justice system was daunting, but I was fortunate to encounter remarkable individuals who stood by me. From the police report to the courtroom, I met dedicated advocates, lawyers, and support workers who believed in me and fought for justice.

Throughout my recovery journey, I came across remarkable mental health professionals. In psych wards, therapy appointments, and group therapy, they provided unwavering guidance and compassion. Although I may not have always appreciated their help at the time, I now recognize the vital role they played in my recovery. However, one remarkable individual stands out – my DBT psychiatrist.

My DBT psychiatrist, your impact on my life has been transforming. Your words, "You don't need to die to solve your problems," became my lifeline. With compassion and your ability, you guided me through my darkest moments, providing me with the necessary tools to help myself and showing that healing and recovery are possible.

Your presence was a turning point, shedding light on my path and empowering me to overcome my past. Every time I achieve something meaningful, I think of you, reminded that you believed in my potential even when I didn't.

Your unwavering faith in my ability to change has left an indelible mark on my heart. I want you to know that your influence continues to inspire me, and I am forever grateful that you saw a future for me when I couldn't. To each and every one of these incredible people, I extend my heartfelt thanks. Your presence in my life, especially during the darkest moments, has been a gift.

My heart will always remember:
- The hands that pulled me out of the water;
- The voices that whispered hope in the darkness;
- The faces that reflected compassion and understanding;
And:
- The hands that let me sink;
- The voices that remained silent;
- The faces that turned away.

Both have shaped me into the person I am today.

To all who have been part of my life, thank you. You mean the world to me. I couldn't have done this without you.

Where To Get Help

Unfortunately, too many people have to experience sexual violence. Every 68 seconds, someone is sexually assaulted or raped, which truly saddens me since no one should ever be forced to go through something they did not choose. You are not alone and there is help out there and there are people who want to listen and be there for you.

Crisis Lines:

- **Suicide crisis helpline: Call or text 988 (24/7)**
- **Manitoba Suicide Prevention & Support Line: 1-877-435-7170 (24/7)**
- **Crisis Text Line Canada: Text 741741 (24/7)**
- **Kids Help Phone: 1-800-668-6868 (24/7), Text 686868**

Domestic Violence and Abuse:

- **National Domestic Violence Hotline Canada: 1-800-363-9010**
- **Assaulted Women's Helpline: 1-866-863-0511**
- **Sexual Assault Crisis Line: (204) 786-8631 (24/7 – Winnipeg) Manitoba Toll Free: 1-888-292-7565**

Online Resources:

- **Crisis Services Canada (online chat support)**
  https://988.ca/
- **BetterHelp Canada (online counselling)**
  https://www.betterhelp.com/
- **Psychology Today Canada (therapist directory)**
  https://www.psychologytoday.com/ca

www.ingramcontent.com/pod-product-compliance
Lightning Source LLC
LaVergne TN
LVHW010928260925
821971LV00006B/234